Making the Matrix Work

Making the Matrix Work

How Matrix Managers
Engage People and
Cut Through Complexity

Kevan Hall

NICHOLAS BREALEY
PUBLISHING

London • Boston

First published in 2013 by Nicholas Brealey Publishing
An imprint of John Murray Press

An Hachette company

9

British Library Cataloguing-in-Publication Data
A catalogue record for this book is available from the British Library.

ISBN 978-1-90483-842-5
eBook ISBN 978-1-90483-843-2

Printed and bound by Bookwell Oy, Finland

John Murray Press policy is to use papers that are natural, renewable and
recyclable products and made from wood grown in sustainable forests.
The logging and manufacturing processes are expected to conform
to the environmental regulations of the country of origin.

Nicholas Brealey Publishing
John Murray Press
Carmelite House
50 Victoria Embankment
London, EC4Y 0DZ, UK
Tel: 020 3122 6000

Nicholas Brealey Publishing
Hachette Book Group
Market Place Center, 53 State Street
Boston, MA 02109, USA
Tel: (617) 523 3801

www.nicholasbrealey.com
www.global-integration.com

Contents

To my wife Diane, and my children Laura and Alan, who admire my jokes and work rate though they try hard to hide it.

1 Introduction

Welcome to the matrix, where multiple bosses, competing goals, influence without authority, and accountability without control are the norm. It is a world where skills, not structure, are the drivers of business and personal success.

At its simplest, a matrix reflects the reality that work no longer fits within the traditional "vertical" structures of function and geography. Today, work is much more "horizontal": it cuts across silos and even extends outside the organization to include suppliers, customers, and other business partners.

Most large organizations now operate some kind of matrix organizational structure in order to serve global customers, coordinate international supply chains, and run integrated internal systems and business functions.

In a matrix, we routinely work with colleagues from different locations, business units, and cultures in cross-functional and virtual teams. Matrix working is now everywhere – and it requires different skills in leadership, cooperation, and personal effectiveness.

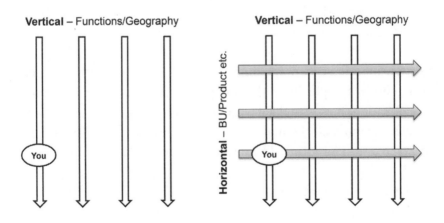

Figure 1.1   From vertical to matrix working

MATRIX ADVANTAGES AND DISADVANTAGES

Matrix management is not the latest management and consulting fad; it has been around since the 1970s. As soon as organizations have multiple locations, countries, or business units that require coordination, some form of matrix evolves, even if only at group level. As organizations become more integrated and share systems, resources, or talent, the matrix evolves so that it reaches deeper into the organization.

Structure should always follow strategy. The four key advantages that organizations seek when introducing a matrix structure are:

- ❏ **To break the silos:** to increase cooperation and communication across traditional vertical silos and to unlock resources and talent that are currently inaccessible to the rest of the organization.
- ❏ **To deliver "horizontal work" more effectively:** to serve global customers, manage supply chains that extend outside the organization, and run integrated business regions, functions, and processes.
- ❏ **To be able to respond more flexibly:** to reflect the importance in the structure of both the global and the local, the business and the function, and to respond quickly to changes in priorities.
- ❏ **To develop broader people capabilities:** a matrix helps us develop individuals with broader perspectives and skills, who can deliver value across the business and manage in a more complex and interconnected environment.

The business logic is compelling, but introducing a matrix does mean a step up in complexity in the way people work together and many organizations have struggled with implementation. Some even claim to have abandoned the matrix (although in reality they usually just move to a simpler form). The disadvantages they cite include:

- ❏ Lack of accountability.
- ❏ Unclear goals and roles.
- ❏ Delays in decision making (too many people getting involved).

❏ Increase in bureaucracy (a proliferation of meetings and committees).
❏ Increase in uncertainty and conflict.

Both the advantages and disadvantages of the matrix are fundamentally about people and the way they work together. Delivering the advantages and avoiding the disadvantages cannot be achieved through a structural change alone, only by building the skills and mindset necessary to cut through the complexity.

A DAMAGING PREOCCUPATION WITH STRUCTURE

Organizations that ignore skills and seek a structural solution on its own can remain stuck in an endless cycle of reorganizations, which not only fail to solve the problem, but make it worse by disrupting the networks and relationships that really get things done.

In my work with over 50,000 people in 300 major multinationals in more than 40 countries, I have learned that structural change solves nothing, and that an excessive focus on structure has been positively damaging to the development of matrix management. Much more important are the networks, communities, teams, and groups that form within a matrix to get things done. Structural change is a blunt, slow, and imprecise tool for forcing change:

❏ It leads to the structure going too deep into the organization. A matrix structure usually only adds value for two or three senior to middle management layers. For the 85 percent or more of people who have purely local jobs (even in the most global organizations), the matrix is likely to cause unnecessary complexity.
❏ It leads to endless reorganizations. Because we are looking for a structural solution to a problem that can only be solved through different skills and ways of working, we keep tinkering with the structure in the vain hope of success.
❏ It leads to a lack of emphasis and underinvestment in building the leadership, collaboration, and individual skills that are vital to make the matrix work.

Skilled people can make almost any structure succeed, but even the most elegant structure will fail if the people within it do not have the skills to make it work.

DELIVERING STRATEGY REQUIRES SKILLS

Effective organizational change flows from strategy to structure to systems to skills. All four waves of change need to be completed and aligned in a successful matrix implementation.

Once organizations are clear about their strategy, they can then focus on the formal structure and the high-level people moves necessary to make their goals happen.

At the same time, many organizations begin a necessary but expensive and time-consuming journey toward common systems. A full-scale SAP, Oracle, or Microsoft Business implementation can take several years and have a major, organization-wide impact on business processes such as product lifecycles, customer relationship management (CRM), supply chain and human capital management. In a large, global organization a full SAP implementation may take five years or more. Depending on the size of your business, and including employee costs, such an implementation could cost tens or even hundreds of millions of dollars.

Nevertheless, many organizations do little beyond announcing the structural changes, and fail to consider how to build the skills to cope with this higher level of complexity. Insufficient thought is given initially to changing criteria for selection and promotion, rewards, capabilities, and training and development to reflect the new environment.

A successful matrix implementation requires the embedding of strategy, structure, systems, *and* skills. A failure to manage change in any of these four areas can lead to a failure of the overall implementation.

In my experience, many organizations invest heavily in structure and systems and neglect the development of skills. When people find it difficult to operate the matrix, they may blame the structure and reorganize again, instead of realizing they lack the necessary skills.

A SHIFT IN POWER FROM STRUCTURE TO SKILLS

Because authority and power are shared between multiple bosses in a matrix, they become less effective as ways of getting things done. Individuals with multiple bosses have to manage tradeoffs and make decisions about where to invest their time and enthusiasm. Managers can feel as if they have lost the authority and control they had in the simpler, functional, single-manager structure of the past.

Two common complaints from managers new to matrix working illustrate this concern:

❑ "How can I be accountable for something I don't control?"
❑ "How can I get things done without authority?"

I will introduce some tools and concepts for dealing with these challenges later, but for now let's think about the implications of these statements. Are these managers really saying that they cannot get things done without direct control and hierarchical authority?

We call the people who raise these objections "matrix victims." Their resistance is often rooted in a lack of confidence in their skills and capability to get things done without traditional control and authority.

In a modern organization, with skilled people, an overreliance on control and power can in fact be counterproductive. It can create unwilling followership at best and is more likely to provoke disengagement, resentment, and avoidance. A hierarchical and control-based individual or corporate culture will really struggle to make a matrix work.

During the implementation of a matrix organization, companies such as IBM and Cisco reported losing around 20 percent of their managers through a combination of structural change and turnover of those who did not fit the new way of working. Most organizations see this turnover as an essential part of bringing about the necessary change in style and embedding matrix behaviors. If your leaders are overreliant on hierarchy and control, they may not be suitable for managing in the matrix.

This shift in power from the structure of the past to the shared authority and more complex skills of the matrix does not go unopposed.

Despite the reality that work has become more horizontal, many organizations have struggled to break the power of vertical silos. Traditionally, authority, control, and power rested in vertical functional and geographic silos; and they still provide the route for career progression for most people. Consciously or unconsciously, powerful vertical managers may resist the loss of power to horizontal processes and reporting lines.

THE EMPLOYEE ENGAGEMENT UPSIDE

While the move from structure to skills can be uncomfortable for managers, it can provide a significant upside in employee engagement, critical in all organizations. High levels of engagement increase "discretionary effort," meaning that people are prepared to go the extra mile to achieve their goals. Greater engagement correlates with high levels of performance, retention, and learning.

Matrix structures often get a bad press for increasing complexity and even conflict, but they do allow us to engage some powerful drivers of employee engagement.

This book will show that matrix success requires individuals to take more ownership of their goals and roles; creates broader and more meaningful jobs; requires higher levels of trust; increases communication and networking; and provides new opportunities for learning and development.

A well-run matrix should enable higher levels of employee engagement. A poorly managed matrix, however, can create matrix victims who feel disempowered in the face of competing goals, lower levels of clarity, multiple bosses, and a more complex working environment.

BUILDING THE SKILLS TO PAY THE BILLS

We cannot expect managers and individuals to be comfortable and effective in this new environment without giving them the skills they need to be successful.

Traditional management prioritizes clarity, predictability, and control. In a matrix, we need to be able to balance this with the ability to tolerate ambiguity, manage change, and decentralize control.

Individuals have been used to clear goals and roles. In a matrix, they need to take more ownership and leadership of their own activities and collaborate with a more diverse and distributed set of colleagues.

People require an expanded toolkit to help them move from the hard to the soft, from the concrete to the ambiguous and back again, depending on the situation. They need to be able to cut through complexity and engage others to get things done.

In this book I will introduce some concepts, tools, and examples to help in four critical areas of matrix leadership and matrix working:

❏ Leading people beyond the limits of clarity.
❏ Streamlining cooperation: being connected and effective.
❏ Getting more control by giving it away.
❏ Building the matrix mindset and skillset.

PART I: LEADING PEOPLE BEYOND THE LIMITS OF CLARITY

Traditional management emphasizes clear goals, roles, and direction. What could be wrong with that?

In a matrix, we deliberately trade some clarity for increased flexibility. We need to balance competing goals and priorities – and the balance required today may be different to the best balance for tomorrow.

I have worked with several organizations that have responded to a matrix structure with lengthy role definitions and ARCI analysis (a process for clarifying roles and job descriptions). At times this can be helpful, but it can also lead to an expectation that the new world is as clear as the old. In a more complex, flexible, and fast-changing environment, can we afford the kind of people who need their boxes to be tightly drawn and who want comprehensive job descriptions, or does this become an unrealistic expectation and an unnecessary constraint?

People want clear goals, but where an individual has multiple bosses, that individual may be the only person to have a full understanding of their role, priorities, and constraints. Goals set in January to be SMART (specific, measurable, achievable, realistic, and time-bounded) may be too simplistic for a complex, fast-changing environment and may be out of date by February.

Matrix managers need to create sufficient clarity and alignment to be effective, and this book introduces tools for doing this. At the same time, we need to give people the ability to manage tradeoffs, dilemmas, and conflicts, as these become more likely in matrix working. If we could completely define and align goals and roles, we would not need a matrix: we could simply cascade our perfect view of the world down from the top.

Employee engagement comes when individuals feel a sense of ownership of meaningful goals, not from rigid job descriptions and goals set by others. By giving people more freedom to shape their goals and their role as well as a greater capability for dealing with ambiguity, we can build even higher levels of ownership, commitment, and engagement.

PART II: STREAMLINING COOPERATION –
BEING CONNECTED AND EFFECTIVE

As we have seen, one of the critical reasons for introducing a matrix is to increase cooperation and communication across traditional silos. To encourage this, companies regularly accompany a matrix implementation with some form of "one company" or "one team" initiative.

But be careful what you wish for! Matrix implementations are often followed by an increase in the number of meetings, conference calls, and emails and a slowdown in the speed of decision making. People become more connected to a wider range of colleagues and reporting lines and the risk is that all of these additional connections invite you to their meetings, copy you on their emails, and involve themselves in your decision making.

At the same time, the cost of cooperation increases sharply. Matrix teams can often involve high levels of travel and more diverse groups of colleagues. Coordinating diaries for meetings, conference calls, and webinars can be a challenge, particularly across time zones.

Normally, economics dictate that when the cost of something increases, the demand for it decreases. However, when we introduce a matrix, often both the cost and the amount of cooperation increase together – and companies rarely budget for these increases in travel, meetings, and communication costs.

In addition, companies typically focus on increasing "teamwork," but teamwork is not the only form of cooperation – and is, in fact, often the most complex and expensive way to organize cooperation within a matrix. There is tremendous value in understanding when teamworking does not add value, as the alternatives can speed up decision making and delivery and improve accountability and job satisfaction.

People who are engaged in what they do enjoy high-quality working relationships with their colleagues, but they also value meaningful work. Nobody enjoys sitting in unnecessary meetings or wading through irrelevant emails. By cutting out unnecessary cooperation, we can create more time to focus on the *critical* relationships and areas of cooperation.

This book will look at four distinctly different ways of cooperating in the matrix: networks, communities, teams, and groups. Each of these four modes of cooperation should be used for specific types of goals; each needs to be established, managed, and engaged differently and should be supported by different types of communication technology. An understanding of the alternatives in cooperation will help you be both connected and effective.

PART III: GETTING MORE CONTROL
BY GIVING IT AWAY

Managers new to the matrix can often find that their trust and confidence in their people are undermined. They are increasingly working with people they do not know well and who they do not have direct control over. They become reliant on others for their success, which many managers find uncomfortable.

Global Integration's clients are leading multinationals and they rarely report a systemic problem with trust. However, there are many factors in matrix working that can subtly undermine trust and confidence: cultural differences and communicating through technology can cause misunderstandings; competing goals can cause conflicts; and a lack of face-to-face time can delay the process of developing trust with new colleagues.

Faced with this environment, many managers, often without making a conscious decision, tend gradually to increase control in an attempt to return to their comfort zone. They introduce more monitoring and reporting, they stay involved in more decisions, and they call more meetings and reviews. Many organizations experience an increase in central control in the period after introducing a matrix.

Centralized control can be very dangerous in a matrix: it leads to high levels of escalation, which can cause delay, additional cost, and dissatisfaction. It can also prevent the very flexibility that we seek in adopting the matrix in the first place.

Decentralized control is faster and more immediate to the situation. By giving away control to the point closest to the action and to the earliest point at which it can be exercised, we build engagement by demonstrating trust and enabling empowerment, and we gain better, faster control.

Many organizations have promoted empowerment and decentralization for decades. In a global matrix we really have no choice, otherwise our leaders will have to make perfect decisions, understand all local cultures, priorities, and situations, and be available 24/7 to deal with escalation and decisions. At best, working in this way will be slow and expensive; in reality, it is unsustainable.

Managers will not empower people they do not trust and trust is a critical component of employee engagement. Trust used to be a free by-product of proximity: we built, maintained, and repaired trust over lunch and after work. Today, we have to structure our activities and relationship building to generate trust quickly and to identify and deal with challenges to trust in a complex, diverse, and distributed world.

Matrix managers need the skills to develop competent and confident people across barriers of distance, culture, time zones, and technology. They also need to find the right balance of trust and control and change it systematically to prevent inflexible central control and to allow people to grow.

When managers are concerned about their ability to deliver accountability without control and influence without authority, we need to give them tools and skills to be effective in an environment where this is completely normal.

PART IV: BUILDING THE MATRIX MINDSET AND SKILLSET

Being successful in this complex working environment requires the "matrix mindset":

❑ **Active self-management:** being a matrix manager (of yourself and others), not a matrix victim.
❑ **Breadth:** taking a perspective and sense of ownership that cut across silos.
❑ **Being comfortable with ambiguity.**
❑ **Adaptability:** being flexible and open to new ideas and ways of working.
❑ **Influencers:** who can establish and engage networks and do not depend on role or authority to get things done.

The development of this matrix mindset is intimately linked to the development of a matrix skillset. There is a saying in training that applies here: "If you're only trained to use a hammer, all of your problems look like nails." If leaders only have a traditional skillset that emphasizes, for example, teamwork and more communication as a solution to everything and insists on complete clarity of goals and roles, they may work very hard to introduce solutions that are in fact counterproductive to developing the skills and engagement levels they need to make the matrix work.

Matrix management represents a significant increase in complexity over the management of traditional organizations, and new skills are required that are adapted to this more complex reality.

A matrix needs to be dynamic and fast changing, and a formal structural response to change is usually too slow. In the future we will increasingly rely on behavioral flexibility and new ways of working to cope with the speed of change we require.

So a matrix does bring higher levels of complexity and ambiguity, but it also brings opportunity. By creating a sense of ownership, autonomy, and personal development, a matrix can create more interesting, fulfilling, and engaging work.

In order to grasp these opportunities, we need to learn some new skills and ways of working, and to unlearn some of the traditional approaches that no longer work.

We will start by looking at how we create clarity and alignment in the matrix, and what to do when we move beyond the limits of clarity into the world of tradeoffs, dilemmas, and conflict.

Part I

Clarity

An organization sets up a matrix because it needs to be good at multiple things at the same time: the global and the local, the function and the business unit. Each of these competes for time, attention, and resources.

The matrix is a deliberate choice to sacrifice some clarity for increased flexibility. In this part I introduce tools and ideas to help individuals manage successively higher levels of ambiguity – from things that can be made clear to managing dilemmas and conflict.

2

Trading
Clarity for Flexibility

The view from the middle

We need clarity in organizations so that we know what we are supposed to be doing and who is supposed to be doing it. We need flexibility to be able to cope with change and complexity.

We set up a matrix organization because we need simultaneously to be good at different things that compete for our time, attention, and money – the local and the global, the function and the business unit, the product and the market. A matrix structure reflects the requirement for both, not one or the other.

Clarity on goals, priorities, and roles is important to employee engagement, but achieving clarity in these areas is always going to be a dynamic process in a fast-changing environment with multiple reporting lines. The balance that gives the right answer today may not be the right answer tomorrow.

If we could create complete clarity and alignment, we would not need a matrix; we could simply publish our objectives and cascade them from the top down.

In this chapter we will see that the issue of clarity looks very different from the top, the middle, and the bottom of the matrix. We will identify the importance of the "matrixed middle" and how different perceptions can undermine trust in management. The chapter covers:

❏ Clarity on WHAT we should be doing
❏ Clarify on HOW we should be doing it
❏ Clarifying the what and the how – life for the matrixed middle
❏ How different perceptions can undermine trust

CLARITY ON *WHAT* WE SHOULD BE DOING

The view from the top

Senior leaders spend a great deal of time discussing the "what" – the goals of the organization. For them, the strategy is clear. They spend months developing the ideas and discussing the options, usually through some form of strategic planning process. They also tend to know each other quite well and have longstanding relationships and networks that allow them to manage conflicts and come up with a broad agreement on what needs to be done.

Senior leaders often think that goals are "clear enough" because they are used to operating in an environment where strategic goals may not always be completely clear. These leaders are accustomed to more ambiguous roles and have a high level of personal and positional power that they can use to get things done.

Because they are comfortable with this kind of environment, senior leaders often underestimate the impact further down the matrix when they expose people to this more ambiguous and flexible world. They can even be frustrated by matrixed middle managers asking for more clarity.

> *Frankly, I am sick and tired of hearing that you are not clear about priorities. I have told you a dozen times what the strategy is! We published it, we have had town hall meetings and we have answered your questions. It is clear! You are experienced people and I expect you to get on with it and stop complaining.*
>
> CEO, global banking in response to question
> from one of his middle managers, UK

If you are right at the top of a matrix organization, then the matrix structure does not really change things that much for you. You are still the boss and everyone still reports to you!

One of the challenges is that senior leaders can underestimate the impact of the matrix on other members of the organization, which can cause problems of perception both ways.

The view from the shop floor

By the time we communicate detailed goals to people in operational roles, we need to make sure that clarity is high or there will be chaos when implementing the plans in manufacturing, retail, and other more structured environments.

At this level, goals should be tangible and measurable. The strategic choices have been made; this is about execution.

The view from the matrixed middle

Managers in the matrixed middle will have competing goals, priorities, and demands on their time.

I agree that my goals are clear. I have a very clear set of goals from my business unit – for example, I know that it is essential to recruit three senior people as quickly as possible to support this year's business plan.

I also have a very clear set of goals from my HR functional line – one of them is to reduce the cost of recruitment. Both are clear, but they are not aligned. The fastest way to recruit would be to use an executive search firm, but that would be the most expensive. So which set of clear goals should I give priority to?
HR business partner, financial services, Singapore

If the strategic goals of the organization are not clear, then managers in the matrixed middle need to escalate decisions to achieve clarity. Senior leaders can help by creating an overall vision that enables prioritization and choice at a high level.

However, matrixed middle managers should not expect 100 percent clarity on their operational goals to be cascaded from on high. In the next chapter we will look at how to create "islands of clarity" by taking ownership for the clarity of our own goals, by seeking out the information we need, and, if it is missing, by starting to create our own clarity.

The matrixed middle also needs the capability, confidence, and information to manage the inevitable tradeoffs and daily dilemmas

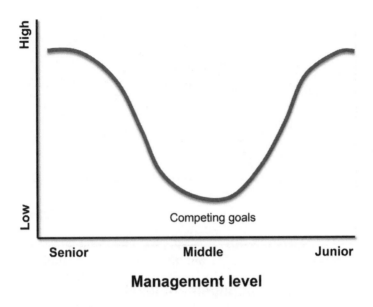

Figure 2.1   Clarity on WHAT we should do

that come from sitting within multiple reporting lines. I will be introducing some tools to help with this in Chapters 6 and 7.

CLARITY ON *HOW* WE SHOULD BE DOING IT

Senior leaders spend much less time on the detail of how the goals and strategies are to be achieved than on the strategy itself.

To a large extent, translating strategy into detailed plans is middle management's job and we cannot expect senior leaders to do this for us – otherwise why do they need middle managers?

So the amount of discussion and even conflict about how things should be done tends to be relatively low at senior management level.

Discussion and conflict about the "how" also tend to be quite low at the operational level, where clear workflow and processes need to be in place to make sure things run efficiently.

Most of the debate and the conflict about how we achieve the strategy happens at middle management level; as indeed it did before we introduced a matrix.

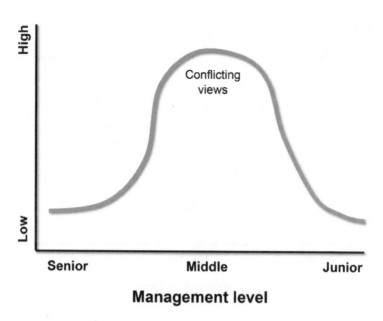

Figure 2.2   Conflict about HOW we should do it

In deciding *how* to do something there is far more scope for opinion, special interests, and personality to cause conflicting views. Resolving these different views and opinions can cause ambiguity and conflict.

In the remaining chapters of Part I we will look at how we can manage this ambiguity or deal with conflict when necessary.

CLARIFYING THE "WHAT" AND THE "HOW" – LIFE FOR THE MATRIXED MIDDLE

Managers in the matrixed middle face a complex environment. Even when the strategy is clear, they will have to deal with competing goals and conflicting views on how that strategy will be achieved. The way they resolve these challenges is essential to the successful working of the matrix.

The matrixed middle will decide on these tradeoffs and dilemmas on a daily basis, unless they choose to escalate issues back up the organization. We need to make sure that they have sufficient knowledge, skills, information, attitude, and confidence to make

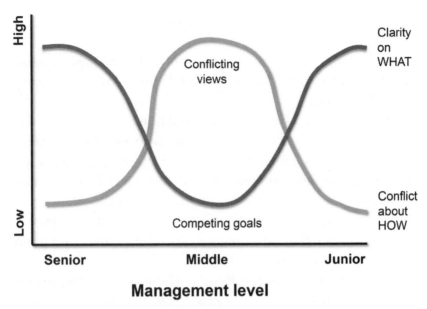

Figure 2.3 The view from the middle

good decisions. The alternative is high levels of escalation or poor judgment calls.

HOW DIFFERENT PERCEPTIONS CAN UNDERMINE TRUST

When I present the clarity curve to corporate audiences, the senior and middle management populations recognize it immediately. It often leads to some wry smiles about the perceptions they secretly hold about each other.

When senior managers look at their middle managers, they often think: "Why don't they get it?" Senior managers faced with complaints and increased amounts of escalation can lose confidence in their middle managers' caliber and capability.

This can lead to senior management frustration and increases in central control to make sure that the things they expect are really happening, which in a matrix can be counterproductive.

Middle managers tend to look at senior managers and say, "Well, of course it looks simple to you, because at your level, it is. It's when you get down to the implementation that it gets complex."

A recent study found that 85 percent of middle managers thought that their roles were unclear, while only 22 percent of senior managers held this view.

Such a perception can undermine middle managers' faith in their senior leaders' willingness to understand the reality they operate in. It also can have an impact on senior managers' willingness to invest in training and skills building, because they tend to underestimate the impact of the matrix on others in the organization.

People at junior levels can lose faith in their middle management population when they see changes in direction, conflict over priorities, and delays in decision making.

The remaining chapters of Part I will focus on equipping managers with the skills and tools they need to take ownership for creating clarity where they can, and to manage dilemmas and conflict when they stray beyond the limits of clarity.

Use the information in this chapter to understand the varying perceptions of clarity at different levels in your organization and how opposing perceptions may undermine trust and confidence in other people.

Before you leave this chapter

❑ Do you recognize these different levels of clarity in your organization?
❑ What perception do these three levels of your organization have of each other?
❑ In what ways would a better understanding of the clarity curve help improve perceptions and understanding of each other's roles?

3

Islands of Clarity

Dealing with competing goals

*Our plans miscarry because they have no aim. When a man does
not know what harbor he is making for, no wind is the right wind.*

Seneca

In any organization it makes sense to have clear goals and
to communicate them clearly to your people. In a matrix,
however, because of multiple reporting lines, a high rate
of change, and a complex environment, goals can compete and
change quickly.

In this chapter I look at what individuals and organizations can
do to make their goals clear. I will also challenge whether traditional
goal-setting and management-by-objectives processes get in the way
of the behaviors needed to be successful in a matrix. I propose tools
that individuals can use to shape their own goals in order to increase
commitment and engagement. The chapter covers:

❑ Matrix goal challenges
❑ Tools that companies use for creating clarity
❑ Creating islands of clarity – shaping your own goals
❑ SMART goals – too simplistic for the matrix?

MATRIX GOAL CHALLENGES

In a matrix there are some additional obstacles to overcome when
clarifying goals:

❏ Goals established by different legs of the matrix may compete for time and attention.

❏ The rate of change tends to be high and goals can quickly become out of date.

❏ Goals can be complex and need to take into account multiple perspectives.

❏ People have limited time together to achieve clarity.

Additional opportunities for misunderstanding come from communicating through technology and from cultural and organizational complexity.

> *I am part of a global marketing organization – I am based in Mexico and responsible for the Mexican market, with a solid line to the market head. Some of our global marketing goals for the year involve standardizing processes and purchasing and adopting key global marketing initiatives. Several of these are probably not perfectly optimized for Mexico. For the same cost, I could deliver something very specific that would have more impact locally. My market head is focused on the Mexico P&L.*
>
> Marketing director, computer hardware, Mexico

> *After the reorganization I now have solid-line reporting to our global IT organization and a dotted line to the country organization. But the reality is my solid-line manager is 3,000 miles away, from a different culture, and I do not know her very well. I know I should be working on important global projects, but the local colleagues I have been working with for years are sitting in front of my desk with an immediate problem. It is tough to say no.*
>
> IT manager, telecommunications, India

TOOLS THAT COMPANIES USE
FOR CREATING CLARITY

Despite this complexity, it makes sense to clarify goals where it is possible to do so.

Organizations use a range of techniques for clarifying goals. The most common are:

❑ Line of sight.
❑ Cascade.
❑ Christmas presents, must-win battles, and fat rabbits.

Line of sight

Here, a great deal of effort is put into making sure that everyone's objectives are clearly aligned to a series of high-level strategic goals. Each individual should be able to see how their personal objectives are directly linked, in "line of sight," to one of the key strategic objectives. This is a relatively bureaucratic process, but can be good if you are trying to achieve some very clear deliverables or to focus the organization on a few imperatives.

> *Our metaphor for our goal-setting process is the lighthouse. Everybody should be clearly able to see a direct line from what they are doing to the overall strategic goals of the business. If it isn't supporting those goals, then they shouldn't be doing it.*
> Operations director, electrical utilities, USA

In reality, though this helps with overall organizational alignment, many of the detailed objectives in the middle of the organization may be only loosely or indirectly connected to very high-level strategic goals. Goal setting in the matrixed middle can become somewhat labored if everything has to be linked explicitly to very high-level goals.

Cascade

Top-down objectives and goals are communicated from the top of the organization through successively lower levels so that everybody understands them and can construct their own goals that link into them.

A cascade resembles a pyramid of champagne glasses: communication is poured into the top and it literally cascades down, filling each glass in turn until it reaches the bottom of the pyramid. There is little opportunity for feedback back up the hierarchy and it can be hard to know whether the message has really been received and understood.

In our business, communication is like turning a hosepipe on a waterlogged field: some parts of the field get even wetter, while some tufts of grass stick out and never even seem to get damp.
Communications specialist, specialty materials, USA

The weakness of the cascade approach rests primarily in a lack of two-way communication. There needs to be an ability to discuss, assimilate, and understand centrally driven objectives, or this merely becomes an exercise in "push" communication that may not really get through to individuals.

We used to have a cascade system in my business, but my boss was not convinced people were actually using the messages in their team meetings. We introduced a mandatory feedback sheet where managers had to identify any key questions with the cascade and we would go back and answer them. It started off as a way of checking that the communication meetings had been held, but ended up creating much more of a dialogue and giving us a reason to go back to line managers with answers to specific questions.
HR manager, fast-moving consumer goods (FMCG), Netherlands

Christmas presents, must-win battles, and fat rabbits

Here, organizations focus on making sure that clarity exists on a small number of extraordinarily important goals. It can be helpful to create some fun or drama around this to increase the impact of the communication.

Christmas is a really important season for us, so our divisional head came up with the idea of giving us a list each January of the

"Christmas presents" he would like in December. We have a big Christmas celebration each year where we symbolically deliver the presents. It sounds a bit corny, but is quite fun and throughout the year it is really clear what we need to deliver and by when.

Purchasing director, FMCG, USA

Our CEO used to be in the military and he uses the terminology of "must win battles." Each year he defines a handful of these and they take precedence over all other goals in the business. He keeps the list small and keeps us focused on the major things we need to achieve.

Commercial director, pharmaceuticals, USA

Prioritization is absolutely essential with this kind of goal. You cannot have 100 top priorities. In our workshops we use the idea that "if an eagle tries to chase two rabbits, both will escape." We get participants to identify which are the "fattest rabbits" on which they are going to focus for that year.

In the majority of cases, when we check with our participants, there is a lack of clarity on the key goals that the organization, division, or department is trying to achieve. Senior managers consistently overestimate how clear the strategy and priorities are to people lower down the organization.

It is worth doing the following exercise at your next meeting or conference call. Ask each individual to write down:

❏ The top three goals of your organization as a whole.
❏ The top three goals of your division.
❏ The top three goals of your department.

Take the time to share these and see whether they are both clear and accurate. You do not need people to be using exactly the same words, but the general understanding should be close enough to allow coordinated action.

It is even more important to be clear and more formal in goal setting in virtual and matrix teams that operate in multiple locations. In a face-to-face environment we cope with unclear goals by having lots of fine-tuning mechanisms. We meet over coffee or lunch, discuss our work, and make constant course changes based on feedback and new information. If we have strayed away from the goals or there is any lack of understanding, this will become clear and our colleagues or boss will bring us back on track.

In a global team, if we leave the kickoff event with any lack of clarity, we can put a great deal of work into the wrong deliverables before it becomes evident to our colleagues that we have misunderstood.

In my last book, *Speed Lead*,® I wrote about the importance of a structured kickoff in a virtual team. An effective kickoff process can reduce the cycle time of virtual teams and projects by 25 percent. It does this by making sure that there is clarity on the key goals, relationships, and ways of working. So an annual "goals kickoff" is a worthwhile routine.

We hold our global team meeting in January. We do a bit of looking back and celebrating the previous year, but mainly we use the opportunity to get focused on our goals for the current year. There is a fair amount of discussion and some peer coaching on our own personal goals. The aim is to leave the meeting completely clear about where we are heading for the year.

VP, global consulting, UK

CREATING ISLANDS OF CLARITY – SHAPING YOUR OWN GOALS

In workshops we regularly hear the complaint from "matrix victims" that they cannot make progress because their goals are not clear and they are waiting for someone else to provide clarity.

Sometimes they are right and their organization has done a poor job of communicating goals; often they are just enjoying a good moan and appear to have little intention of doing anything about it!

In a traditional hierarchical organization, we expect that goals will be cascaded down through the authority structure. In a matrix, the reality is that we may have competing goals or a lack of clarity on priorities. If we wait for this to be resolved centrally by someone else, we can expect the resolution to be slow at best and it will probably never happen.

For this reason, we need to take personal responsibility for creating clarity in our own goals. In a matrix, if our goals are not clear, it is up to us to make them so.

This may turn out to be a positive advantage in creating employee engagement: people tend to be more committed to goals that they choose for themselves than to ones that were set by others. Whatever our situation, it is usually possible to create clarity in some areas of our goals.

Follow these three steps to create your own islands of clarity:

- ❏ Clarify your routine goals.
- ❏ Identify the specific questions you need answering.
- ❏ Create your own proposals.

Clarify your routine goals

Many people's goals are remarkably consistent year after year. Each of us has certain activities that will need to be completed time and again:

- ❏ Finance people will need to complete planning and budgeting processes and produce accounts.
- ❏ HR people will need to conduct appraisal, training needs, recruitment, and succession processes.
- ❏ Supply-chain people will need to acquire, store, manufacture, and move products.

In most roles these activities create a structure to the goals and they are reasonably consistent over time. Start by creating clear goals in these areas.

It is safe to assume that each year you will be asked to perform these activities faster, to a higher level of quality, at a lower level of cost!

Identify the specific questions you need answering

Once you have done so, approach the people who can help you resolve them.

The simplest process I have ever seen for doing this was used by one of our clients:

We used to have a problem with people complaining that there was a lack of clarity. So at the end of each meeting we created a flipchart with two columns – "what is now clear" and "what is still not clear." For the items that were not clear, we allocated someone to go and find out. At the beginning of the next meeting, we reported back.

It helped clear up most of the issues. Although we ourselves were sometimes not clear, other people in the business often were or could help us work through the options. There were still a couple of things that weren't clear and when we escalated them we were told "those are your decisions to make," which was also helpful.

There is sometimes a tendency to complain about clarity and assume that someone else should be providing it. If you take charge of your own information needs, a lot of things can be resolved quite quickly.

R&D leader, specialty materials, Germany

Create your own proposals

Talk to the key stakeholders in your goal areas and get their views. Discuss with your managers and your team and make your own proposals on goals in these areas.

Publish your draft goals to your managers and ask for comments. If you are wrong they will respond and tell you why, but at least you have begun to shape your goals, rather than waiting for them to be set by somebody else who, in a matrix, may have a less accurate understanding of your full role than you do.

Create a list of items that are still not clear and review them regularly with your team.

By creating your own "islands of clarity" in the areas where you have the ability to do so, you are beginning to shape your own situation. Because you developed the goals yourself, they are likely to be more meaningful to you and you are likely to be more committed to delivering them.

Once you have done this, you are in a stronger position to push back at the people around you who may not have the same level of clarity.

Shaping the choices

If goals are not clear in the matrixed middle, the people at the heart of multiple reporting lines, then those people will make their own choices.

This can be a positive advantage to engagement, leading to higher levels of ownership and commitment. Nevertheless, there is also a risk that some individuals will prioritize goals that are most interesting or enjoyable to them personally or that they may follow the line of least resistance or the leg of the matrix that shouts loudest.

If we want people to be able to make the correct decisions around their own goals and priorities, we have to make sure that we give them sufficient context and information on what they need to do when objectives are unclear.

Most traditional management textbooks tell us that we do this by having a clear vision. While this is always important, most corporate visions are written at such a high level that they do not enable us to choose clearly between competing operational priorities.

An overall direction, roadmap, or vision of where the organization is heading is useful, but it is normally not sufficient to enable us to resolve competing goals. If we lack even that basic sense of direction, however, we really are in trouble.

Organizations can also use clear values and ways of working to shape important choices by defining acceptable business practices and behaviors.

SMART GOALS – TOO SIMPLISTIC FOR THE MATRIX?

In traditional performance management, goal setting is the beginning of a process of management by objectives. We set goals and measures that are linked to our performance-evaluation and reward systems.

This tends to be quite a linear process and is relatively inflexible. It tends to assume a 12-month visibility of goals that will not change.

I was quite proud at the end of the year with what I had achieved. There had been a lot of change in the business during the year and I had to be really flexible to make sure that I did the right thing. I was astounded when my director complained that I had not met three of the objectives that were set in January.

Business priorities had changed and what I had actually achieved was of far more value to the business. His view, however, was that my goals were my commitments and, as I hadn't formally changed them with him during the year, that was what he was expecting me to deliver. Well, at least I will know what to focus on next year!

Logistics manager, electronics, Germany

As a junior manager I was successful by focusing on my goals and metrics. This business is very focused on metrics. I was recently promoted to executive level and am now working in a matrix. Now I have to make decisions on tradeoffs and priorities. This may mean that the right thing to do is miss my numbers to help someone hit a more important set of numbers. Unfortunately, this will count against me under our system.

Executive, global industrial group, USA

SMART goal setting recommends goals that are specific, measurable, achievable, realistic, and time bounded. In a fast-changing environment where priorities change and complex issues evolve over time, this may be oversimplistic.

Performance management in a matrix needs to pay attention to people's ability to juggle competing priorities, make decisions on tradeoffs, and be prepared to give up their goals in order to help others achieve more important objectives. Goal setting, metrics, and performance evaluation will look very different if we are trying to encourage these matrix-mindset behaviors.

Perhaps the fundamental problem is that we are trying to drive too much from our goal-setting process. We are using goals to drive direction on prioritization, but also to make decisions on performance management, rewards, and career development. In a simpler and more linear world this was already a challenge. In the complex world of the matrix, we need to be more realistic and more discerning about how we make such complex decisions about people.

Part of the issue of achievement is to be able to set realistic goals, but that's one of the hardest things to do because you do not always know exactly where you're going, and you shouldn't.

George Lucas

Use the information in this chapter to create your own islands of clarity and make your goals clear where possible.

In Chapter 12 I will return to this theme and provide some additional information on finding the right balance of accountability and control in goal setting.

Before you leave this chapter

❏ Are your personal goals clear?
❏ If not, what specific information do you need to make them clear? Who can help you with this?
❏ Have you created your "islands of clarity"?
  • Clarify your routine goals.
  • Identify the specific questions you need answering.
  • Create your own proposals.
❏ Does your goal-setting and performance-management system reinforce the behaviors you need to be successful in a matrix?

4

Owning Your Role

Clarifying roles and decision rights

Research shows that role clarity is highly correlated with engagement, performance, and retention, so it is important to get this right.

However, roles in a matrix are broader and more ambiguous than those in simpler organizations. A tightly drawn job description, written by someone else, sends the wrong message when we are looking for flexibility and encouraging people to take ownership for their own roles and think across the silos.

In this chapter I will focus on creating role and decision clarity where that is possible. The chapter covers:

❏ The problem with roles
❏ ARCI in the matrix
❏ Critical questions in role clarity
❏ Clarifying decision rights
❏ Do-it-yourself role clarity

THE PROBLEM WITH ROLES

In a recent study, 85 percent of employees stated that they didn't have a clear understanding of the responsibilities or duties required of them to carry out their job or the expectations of their manager for how they should fulfill their responsibilities.

Another study claimed that 64 percent of performance-related issues stemmed from employees' lack of understanding of the requirements of their role.

This is a critical issue for engagement. How can we hope to build a sense of meaning and an emotional connection to roles that we do not understand?

I am a project manager, but also a mom with a son who loves hockey. I was at a hockey match recently and one mom was always shouting at her son: "Get in there where the puck is, get involved, get in there." After a while I got irritated with this and asked her: "What position does your son play?"

She answered: "He plays on the wing."

"Well, surely his job is to stay out wide in space so that people can find him, attack and go forward? If everyone chases the puck then no one is in space, no one is thinking strategically, no one is available for that attacking move."

It can be like that at work too: are we all chasing the puck, are we all getting involved, or is somebody thinking strategically, making sure they do their own work and metaphorically staying out on the wing to allow the attacking move when it is possible?

Project manager, chemicals, USA

Before we focus on role clarity, do not forget that the nature of a matrix is ambiguous, with competing goals and the need for high levels of flexibility. We should *expect* roles to be less clear in a matrix than in a traditional organization. Roles are more likely to cross organizational boundaries, to involve more people, and to have to incorporate more perspectives and stakeholders. This brings the opportunity to build broader and more engaging roles and to learn new perspectives and skills, but at the risk of additional complexity.

I have noticed in our training workshops that, despite people accepting the idea of ambiguity intellectually, when we give them role-clarity tools they immediately forget it and put enormous effort into trying to get back to perfectly clear and defined roles.

I worked with a client in the Nordic region who wanted more clarity on roles:

*Since we introduced a matrix two years ago, we have put a tre-
mendous amount of effort into a role-sort exercise to clarify roles,
in particular some organizational interfaces between marketing
departments. We've tried several ways of doing this, but still have
some persistent challenges. Do you have any new tools we can use
to help with this?*

HR manager, FMCG, Sweden

My view was that if they had been unable to resolve this lack of ambiguity in two years, then perhaps this was a clue that they were searching for a clarity that no longer existed.

We should also recognize that role clarity is deeply personal. It
is a subjective feeling of having or not having as much clearness as
you would like to have. Because of this, it will vary widely among
different individuals. What is hopelessly unclear to one person may
be clear enough to another.

*There are known knowns: there are things we know that we
know. There are known unknowns: that is to say, there are things
that we now know we do not know. But there are also unknown
unknowns – there are things we do not know we do not know.*

Donald Rumsfeld, US Secretary of Defense

*I do not want my role to be defined too clearly. I like the opportu-
nity to be involved in a range of issues and to focus on what I think
are the priorities or the biggest opportunities in the business, rather
than have a tightly defined set of activities and deliverables. I also
find "it is easier to ask for forgiveness than permission," so I just get
on with what I think needs doing.*

Business planning manager, FMCG, Australia

Role clarity is also about access to information. An issue may not be
unclear to the organization as a whole, but if you are missing a critical perspective or piece of information it may be unclear to you personally. Many ambiguities can be resolved by seeking out the person
who does have the answer to these questions.

However, do not let the perfect stand in the way of the good. The complexity of a matrix means that it is often better to make progress with "good enough" clarity rather than spending inordinate amounts of time trying to drive out every ambiguity.

ARCI IN THE MATRIX

The most-used tool for achieving role clarity in organizations is some version of an ARCI analysis. I will start with a simple definition of the tool and then explain some of the specific complexities of applying this in a matrix.

You may find the same process referred to elsewhere as RACI; ARCI may be a less appealing acronym, but it is more accurate in describing the sequence.

In an ARCI analysis we define, for a particular task or area of responsibility, who is accountable, responsible, consulted, or informed in delivering that task successfully. More complex versions may include additional roles such as supporting, verifying, or approving the activity.

Role	Simple definition
Accountable	This role is held fully accountable for the delivery of the task.
Responsible	This role conducts the actual work or owns the problem.
Consulted	This role has the information and/or capability to complete the work. There is two-way communication (typically between R and C).
Informed	This role is to be informed of progress and results. There is one-way communication (typically from R to I).

If you search the internet for "RACI" you will quickly find many worked examples, charts, and spreadsheets online that will give you more information if you need it.

What is different about ARCI in the matrix?

Being clear about these respective roles and who does what can help eliminate many issues around role clarity. The simple definition of ARCI, however, has to be adapted to the more complex environment of a matrix.

Who is Accountable?

In traditional ARCI analysis, the assumption is that only one person should be accountable for a major basket of work or area of responsibility. This is a great principle, but the whole design of a matrix means that accountabilities will often be shared.

Because of this, we need to be clear about how we resolve issues at the level of accountability: will disagreements be escalated, will one leg of the matrix have a tie-breaker vote, or can we break down accountabilities into smaller subaccountabilities so that they can be more clearly assigned?

In a matrix we rarely have full control over the things we are accountable for. We rely on a network of supporting functions and colleagues to deliver their accountabilities; without them, we may not be able to achieve what we have to on our own. In Chapter 12 I will come back to the issue of accountability without control in more detail.

In our matrix we have given the "host manager" primary responsibility for driving local communication, the performance evaluation process, and functional development. Individuals also work on cross-functional teams and projects and the "activity manager" provides the input on performance evaluation, handles any activity-specific communication and any training specific to the needs of the project or activity. In performance evaluation and personal development, both need to agree on a plan for the year and one cannot complete the activity without the other.

HR director, biotechnology, Belgium

Usually the trick is to get down to a sufficient level of detail, where the accountabilities become clearer.

If too many people are identified as "accountable" for a task, this will normally cause confusion. Try to keep as few people as possible at this level: one is still optimal, but may be hard to achieve in the matrix.

If you find that one individual has too many accountabilities, this may be a sign that you have created a bottleneck or that too many issues are being escalated for resolution.

Who is Responsible?

The second category is to define who is responsible. These are the people who do the work.

There will often be many people involved in doing the work in a matrix, although it is important to keep this number manageable.

If there are too many people in the "responsible" box, this can be an indicator that there is too much role overlap in the organization. If the same people appear as responsible for too many tasks, this may be an indicator of task overload.

If you find that some roles are lacking in accountabilities or responsibilities, then those roles probably do not add much value to the organization and may need to be removed.

Who needs to be Consulted?

It can be very valuable to make clear the role of the C in ARCI. "Consult" means that you ask for and listen to someone's opinions and inputs before you make a decision – it does not mean that they are the decision maker or that they have to agree.

In a matrix there is a tendency for too many Cs to be involved – everyone believes that they should be consulted on everything.

These people are often best engaged on a one-to-one basis or in an initial kickoff meeting only. If you invite them to regular meetings, you may find them adding a wide range of opinions and perspectives, which can get in the way of reaching a consensus. They may also feel that they should attend future meetings and get more deeply involved in the decision process. ARCI can help you be specific about the overall level of involvement of the people you consult.

Who needs to be Informed?

As with Cs, make sure that the role of Is is clear. "Inform" means that when you have made a decision you will tell this person about it. Again, it does not mean that they are the decision maker or have a right of veto. You are not asking them for other forms of involvement or approval.

This may seem a little harsh, but it is important to be clear, otherwise there is a tendency for more people to become engaged in the process than are necessary, which can lead to delays and additional costs in decision making and delivery of the activity.

If you find roles that contain very high levels of "consult" and "inform" activities without any real accountabilities or responsibilities, then you should check that you have not created unnecessary roles or information flows that are adding little value.

Patterns to watch for

Pattern	In tasks	In roles
Too many As	Interference and confusion	Unclear organizational structure
Too many Rs	Overlaps of roles	Overwork
No Rs or As	Gaps in the system or unnecessary work	Is this role necessary?
Too many Cs and Is	Unnecessary information flows	Is this role necessary?

There are some additional challenges in the application of ARCI in a complex environment.

Most organizations find conducting a full ARCI analysis of the roles in their organization extremely time consuming.

We found it very useful to do the RACI analysis, but it took a lot of time and effort to complete, and as soon as we completed it we started to find things that we had not anticipated. Objectives and priorities changed, and it seemed like a lot of work to go back over that whole process again. We worked out that it only made sense to do RACI from time to time, maybe once a year or at a time of major organizational change, rather than something you keep as a living document.

Project manager, engineering, Brazil

More fundamentally, the analysis may even be sending the wrong message to individuals. If you are the kind of person who wants their role box to be tightly drawn and absolutely clear, a matrix may not be the right kind of working environment for you.

I do not think I ever had an up-to-date job description during my corporate career; it would have been perceived as negative even to ask for one.

We may do individuals a disservice by encouraging them to think that complete clarity is either attainable or desirable. We want people in the matrix to have a more flexible mindset, so we should allow, or perhaps even insist on, some ambiguity.

For this reason, I would recommend using ARCI by exception only on specific cases and to resolve escalations. If there are particular issues that are regularly escalated for decisions to senior management, this may be an indicator of lack of role clarity. Similarly, role or interorganizational conflicts may be caused by unclear boundaries. In these cases, we may apply ARCI by exception to resolve these specific problems. This prevents us from putting unnecessary effort and bureaucracy into areas where roles are already clear enough.

Although not strictly part of the ARCI analysis itself, we can gain some useful information from the discussions that lead to its completion. For example, we may identify areas where the wrong people are involved in activities and decisions, or where issues and decisions are incorrectly escalated.

We may also identify certain behaviors that we need to change in ways of working in this area. We should add this information to the bottom of the ARCI analysis so that we remember to work on the root causes or legacy behaviors that have contributed to the lack of clarity in this area in the past.

CRITICAL QUESTIONS IN ROLE CLARITY

Another way of identifying problem areas with role clarity is to see whether people can answer certain critical questions. Each of the categories represents an area where ambiguity can creep into a role.

❏ **Are you clear about what you are expected to deliver?** This needs to be checked with multiple stakeholders and multiple team members, so that expectations are clear and shared.

❏ **Are you clear about how you are expected to work?** That might be the work methods or processes, but it also might be the style of behavior expected, or the information you need to be able to do your job.

❏ **Are you clear how to prioritize?** What information, authority, or skills do you need in order to be able to prioritize activities and goals?

❏ **Do you understand the consequences and implications of your role for others?** Have you understood the network of inter-relationships necessary to be successful and the boundaries and role interfaces that need to be managed?

Rather than have these areas defined in detail by managers, we recommend that individuals go out and find the answers to these questions themselves. By doing so, they create a higher level of understanding of their roles and others' expectations, they can negotiate any unrealistic expectations, and they create the sense of ownership for their own role that is critical to employee engagement.

Roles in a matrix can rarely be seen in isolation; they need to be understood in the context of other roles with which they coordinate and to whom they provide service or information.

We recently moved from a vertical business line organization to a matrix where I now have business partners in HR and IT as part of my team, who also serve other parts of the organization. It wasn't really clear to me how much time they have available to dedicate to my team, so I wanted to make expectations clear and shared.

I got each of the team members to present their accountabilities and roles on a flipchart to their colleagues on the team. Interestingly they also added, spontaneously, a couple of points that they were not accountable for (particularly those issues that people thought they should deliver but were not part of their role).

It was a useful process. We each shared our accountabilities followed by a discussion for understanding. We found a couple of things that didn't need doing, but more importantly we got a good understanding of how much we could really expect from our colleagues who are only partly dedicated to the team.

It is something we plan to repeat from time to time so we can understand our team members' total accountabilities and not just the subset of them that we see on a daily basis.

VP, insurance, Hungary

Three issues that people worry about in role clarity

I have been focusing on how individuals can make the elements of their role clear enough to be successful. However, there are also some typical issues that people are concerned about in reaching a true understanding of their roles.

❑ **Who is my boss?** Who decides on pay, career, and performance evaluation? In a matrix this will often be shared, but we do need to make the process and responsibilities clear in relation to how this will work and who will do what.

As one of our participants once said as we left for a break, after a session on virtual working, "If you see my boss during the break, could you tell me who it is?"

Manager, telecoms, Netherlands

❑ **What control do I have over resources?** In a sense this is the wrong question, because control over resources is always shared in a matrix organization and concerns about control are often a symptom of either a lack of trust or a lack of skills to enable things to get done without traditional authority.

41

I was promoted into an EMEA matrix role and asked my boss how many people were on my team. He answered, "There is good news and bad news. The good news is there are around 300 people on your team. The bad news is that none of them know it yet and they will all continue to report to other people."

Business planning manager, FMCG, France

❏ **If something goes wrong, who is accountable?** If people are routinely asking this question in your organization, it may again be a symptom of a lack of trust, confidence, or skills. There are, however, some skills and tools that can help in managing this in a matrix environment. We will spend more time in Part III on trust and accountability without control.

These questions illustrate how deeply people remain concerned with traditional issues of hierarchy and control. We need to provide individuals with sufficient clarity in these areas for them to operate successfully. But we must also build an understanding that getting comfortable with high levels of ambiguity and shared authority and control is absolutely critical to the success of the matrix.

CLARIFYING DECISION RIGHTS

A regular issue in matrix workshops is clarity of decision rights. Matrix working tends to be more collaborative. If we are not clear about who will be involved in decisions and the process that will be followed, there can be a tendency for more people than are necessary to be involved and for the process to become slow and bureaucratic.

Using the ARCI process can often help with this. If you need to focus more on decision making specifically, then you may want to add an additional category, D = decision maker.

It is also useful to understand the decision-making process itself — the mechanisms that will be used to make a decision.

In simple terms, there are four ways of making decisions:

❏ **The boss decides.** This is a decision that should be made on the basis of authority. It could be defined in the organization's rules for delegation of authority, or it may be something the boss feels the need to reserve to him- or herself.

❏ **Collegiate decisions.** In this style of decision making the boss will consult others, but is responsible for making the final decision.

> *Occasionally, our chief executive would use what he called "collegiate" decision making. He was always very clear: "This is my call, but I want to hear, from each of you, your honest opinion on what we should do."*
>
> *It sounds as though it could have been disempowering, but he didn't do it very often and actually we all knew our roles and were able to speak our minds, knowing that he would make the final decision.*
>
> VP, power engineering, Switzerland

❏ **An empowered individual decides.** The decision is within the area of responsibility of an expert or someone with specific responsibility for this and that individual is confident and empowered to make the decision. These decisions are made on the basis of expertise or role.

❏ **Collective decisions.** The decision-making unit is more than one person and therefore there needs to be a process of discussion and agreement. Most commonly, groups decide either through consensus (everyone discusses and comes to a common view) or some form of voting (formal or informal), where the majority view holds sway. These decisions are a collective process, which may again be based on expertise and role rather than hierarchy or formal authority.

In clarifying decision rights, it is important to be clear about who needs to be involved and which of these processes they will use to make a decision.

In a healthy matrix, decision making should be able to flow to the individuals who have the expertise to make the decision, rather than merely to the person with positional authority.

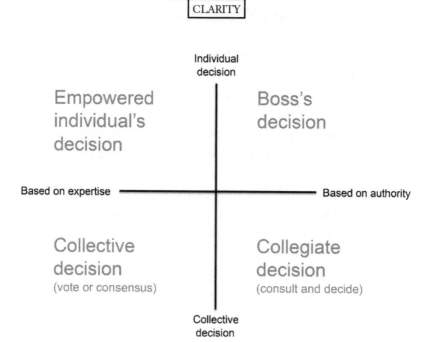

Figure 4.1   Decision making – expertise vs. authority

"Why talk to someone with a job title, when you can talk to someone with an answer?"

Sales manager, specialty materials, USA

In the absence of this clarity, there is a tendency to default to collective decision making, which is relatively slower and more complex. There are times when this is the right way to make decisions, but there are many more occasions when empowered individuals will get the job done better and faster.

There are also some dangers in collective decision making in areas where expertise should be the primary criterion.

I sit on a team with a number of specialists in areas like regulatory affairs, medical, market access, and marketing. It seems as though the team has become the decision-making body for everything. One symptom of this is that we cannot seem to make a decision in between meetings. In some cases, I find myself voting on a proposal made by the content expert in a particular area. It cannot

*be right that the average of the views of the one person who does
know and the six who do not is the way the decisions are taken!*
Medical director, pharmaceuticals, Turkey

DO-IT-YOURSELF ROLE CLARITY

Some individuals seem to want a perfectly clear role defined by their
boss. However, in an environment with multiple bosses, you may be
the only person who has a full understanding of all aspects of your
role.

The more bosses you have, the more you will need to be proactive
and take the initiative to achieve role clarity for yourself. While this
may seem like extra work, it does give you an opportunity to shape
your role according to your own interests and beliefs about what
needs doing. This is likely to increase your engagement in and commitment to the role.

It is quite common in workshop sessions for matrix victims to say,
"This is great stuff, but do our senior managers know this? When
will they resolve this ambiguity? When will they make things clear?"

If things are not clear in your role, then you are the person with the
most knowledge and hopefully the most motivation to sort this out.

One of my favorite sayings is: "If not you, then who? If not now,
then when?" You cannot wait for senior managers to achieve clarity,
because for them things may already be clear enough.

Use ARCI and the other tools and questions in this chapter to
clarify elements of your role where you can. Engage with your key
stakeholders to discuss their expectations of your role. Share your
role and accountabilities with your colleagues to make sure that
expectations and boundaries are clear. In the process, you will learn
a great deal about your role and how it is perceived and begin to take
real ownership for shaping your role in the future.

At the same time, be aware that not everything will be clear in
a matrix. In the next few chapters we look at dealing with factors
that are much less clear: managing dilemmas, tradeoffs, ambiguity,
and even conflict. All of these are completely normal in a matrix and
managing them well is essential to success.

Before you leave this chapter

❑ What elements of your role are not clear?
❑ Who can help you to clarify these areas?
❑ Would an ARCI analysis help?
❑ Can you answer the critical questions on role clarity?
❑ Are decision rights clear in your role and team?
❑ Are you clear about the roles of close colleagues, and do they understand your role?

5

Getting Aligned
with Others

Aligning on a moving target

A lack of alignment of goals and roles is one of the most common complaints in matrix working. Lack of alignment can lead to duplication, confusion, and wasted effort.

At the same time, it is important to recognize that if we could be perfectly aligned we would not need a matrix: we could just cascade everything down from the top.

In this chapter I will introduce some tools and ideas for creating alignment between horizontal and vertical elements within your own role, aligning with others in the matrix, and managing competing goals. The chapter covers:

❑ The alignment challenge
❑ Creating organizational alignment
❑ Aligning goals within your own role
❑ Managing competing goals
❑ Aligning your goals and role with others in the matrix

THE ALIGNMENT CHALLENGE
....

Global Integration's matrix and virtual teams benchmarking survey enables individuals and teams to compare themselves with over 4,000 other individuals who work in such complex teams in more than 40 leading global organizations. Here are the percentages of people agreeing or strongly agreeing with the following statements about goals and alignment:

- ❏ My personal goals and objectives within the team are clear to me – 84 percent
- ❏ I know and understand the goals and objectives of others in the team – 72 percent
- ❏ The objectives of team members do not conflict with each other – 73 percent

As you would expect, people are clearer about their own goals than those of others. However, if 16 percent are not clear about even their own goals and nearly 30 percent of team members do not understand the goals of others in the team or consider that these goals actively conflict with each other, then this is a serious problem.

Some symptoms of alignment issues include the following:

- ❏ **High levels of escalation.** If the legs of the matrix are not well aligned, individuals further down the organization will find it difficult to resolve priority or goal conflicts. They will escalate these to senior managers for resolution.
- ❏ **Repeated poor judgment calls.** If individuals regularly seem to make poor decisions when managing tradeoffs and priorities, it is likely that they do not have access to the information, knowledge, or skills necessary to make accurate judgments.
- ❏ **Gaps or overlaps.** If there are regular gaps in results or duplicated work in the organization, this may be a clue that there is insufficient alignment.
- ❏ **Resource disputes.** All organizations have limited resources. If individuals further down the matrix are unable to resolve disputes about competition for resources or if these disputes regularly become heated, it may be a symptom of misalignment.
- ❏ **Unsynchronized processes.** Particularly in the early stages of moving to a matrix, rewards, budgets, and other systems may be aligned to legacy ways of working and may cause conflicts with matrix goals and roles.

In many cases these are symptoms of poor communication and coordination: one part of the organization does not know what the other part is doing.

While I will highlight some tools for creating alignment in this chapter, it is equally important to have a live mechanism for resolving the inevitable alignment issues that arise in matrix working.

> *We used to get a lot of escalation to the functional managers when we first introduced matrix teams. An individual would go along to, let's say, their commercial functional head with a conflict between the commercial function goals and the matrix team goals. The commercial head, of course, reiterated that the commercial goals were to have precedence. We found out that escalating serious issues up only one leg of the matrix was unproductive.*
>
> *Now it is mandatory to escalate to both legs of the matrix, so both commercial and matrix team heads get together to hear the issue and look for a solution. We find we get fewer escalations that way, but also that we are more likely to get a resolution.*
>
> Matrix team leader, advertising, Hong Kong

Alignment isn't only a rational matter of objectives and roles, there is also an emotional component. In global organizations, for example, particularly in the early stages of a matrix implementation, people tend to be pulled more strongly toward their local goals by their legacy relationships and shared history, culture, and language.

Even though, intellectually, individuals usually understand the need to be global and to integrate across regions and share resources, there remains an emotional alignment toward local relationships and activities. In *Speed Lead* I called this "divided loyalty" and looked at some of the "keys to community" that we can use to bridge this gap, such as building a shared culture and values or changing compensation.

At one conference, when attempting to illustrate some of the pitfalls of matrix working, I gave two people pieces of string tied to my hands and asked them to try to get me to complete a physical task. They both tried to pull me in their direction using the string. This represents how it can feel being at the intersection of two or more legs of the matrix.

If there is insufficient alignment, then goals and reporting lines will be pulling you in different directions. If your goals pull in opposite directions, you do not go anywhere – you put all of your effort into resisting being pulled in half!

The quickest way to resolve the exercise with the strings is either to get the "managers" perfectly aligned, or to give the individual at the intersection of the strings the information and authority to make a decision for themselves.

Perfect alignment may be impossible or even undesirable; we introduced a matrix in the first place because we have competing objectives and demands on our time. Resources and priorities have to be balanced, not permanently resolved in favor of one or the other.

Indeed, if we were perfectly aligned, why would we need a matrix? In our strings exercise above, if both managers are pulling in exactly the same direction, why do we need two of them?

The more passionate the people we employ are, the more likely they are to have different views about priorities and the right way to do things. Alignment is not about driving this passion out of the organization, but about giving people the information and the skills they need to discuss and resolve those disagreements in a positive way.

If we can achieve high levels of alignment, we may reduce the need for a formal matrix structure. The following example, from a Netflix presentation on culture, shows how this media company aspires to be highly aligned but loosely coupled – a nice distinction:

Highly aligned
❏ Strategy and goals are clear, specific, broadly understood.
❏ Team interactions focus on strategy and goals, rather than tactics.
❏ Requires large investment in management time to be transparent and articulate and perceptive.

Loosely coupled
❏ Minimal cross-functional meetings except to get aligned on goals and strategy.
❏ Trust between groups on tactics without previewing/approving each one – so groups can move fast.
❏ Leaders reaching out proactively for ad hoc coordination and perspective as appropriate.
❏ Occasional post mortems on tactics necessary to increase alignment.

CREATING ORGANIZATIONAL ALIGNMENT

There are many books on strategic and organizational alignment, which tend to focus on high-level strategy. If organizations are not aligned at a strategic level, then it is extremely hard to align goals and roles at the tactical level.

Organizational alignment usually includes the following areas.

Strategic alignment

Organizations develop and communicate their vision, mission, and key strategies. Individuals align their goals to the vision and strategy through "line of sight" or other tools (see Chapter 3 on goal clarity). There should also be a feedback mechanism by which individuals inform the strategic debate with their learning and experiences of implementation.

Balanced scorecard

Robert S Kaplan and David P Norton, in their book *The Balanced Scorecard*, popularized the concept of creating strategy maps, scorecards, and dashboards to create alignment throughout an organization.

Balanced scorecards were originally based around four categories of synergy: financial, customer, internal processes, and learning and growth. All of these should be focused on creating value across the enterprise and should flow from the overall vision and strategy of the business. In each of the four areas we identify objectives, key measures, targets, and activities or initiatives designed to drive success in that particular area.

The concept has since been developed to include a wide range of financial and nonfinancial measures, with the idea of keeping organizations focused on key and very visible initiatives and measures through some form of "digital dashboard."

The balanced scorecard can be extended to include external organizations such as suppliers, customers, and partners in order to help build shared understanding and common metrics of success.

These can then be cascaded throughout the organization, so that each business unit or department can create its own scorecard and dashboard based on the top-level strategic ones.

According to consultants Bain & Co., by 2004 57 percent of global companies were using some form of balanced scorecard. You can find some worked examples online with a web search on "balanced scorecard."

Common "values" and culture

A strong shared culture can help individuals make qualitative decisions about how they should respond to given situations.

My organization has a strong culture based around five principles. These are at a fairly high level, but the language is regularly used in the business to solve problems. If I am in a situation where I am not entirely clear about the right response, I know that if I fall back on the values my decisions will be supported by my managers and colleagues. An enduring solution needs to be consistent with our culture to work.

Purchasing manager, food industry, USA

One of our key values is that our business relationships should be mutual – everyone should see the benefits if we want the relationship to endure. That means that we are always looking for ways to add value and share the benefits – a solution where all the value accrues to one partner or the other isn't a good solution.

VP, global consulting, UK

A number of leading organizations are now using what is known as graphic facilitation to create an overall metaphor or image to align their people.

We used a graphic facilitator to create an image that represented our strategic journey toward geographic expansion in Asia and the issues and barriers around achieving it. The image was of a fleet of ships leaving Denmark and heading to Asia. Hopefully we look more like explorers than Viking raiders!

We included all the key preparation stages for the "voyage" in the image, issues of navigation and supply on the journey, weather and tides (things that could help or hinder us), and the main challenges that we would have to overcome on landing.

The image and the metaphor worked really well in creating a common understanding of the issues and were particularly helpful in communicating to a wider audience.

We have been able to update the image as the journey has progressed and post copies of it around our offices. It is a really useful unifying metaphor for what we are trying to achieve.

Communications director, healthcare, Denmark

You can see an example of a graphic template in action by searching for "Speed Lead" on YouTube.

Cross-business campaigns

In large, diversified businesses with different strategies and priorities, one way of creating alignment and a sense of common purpose is to use initiatives that cross all business units and geographies and unite them in a common enterprise and learning.

GE is an organization of nearly 300,000 employees in over 160 countries. It incorporates many different types of industry, from financial services to consumer products and from energy to healthcare.

GE routinely creates campaigns on themes such as "boundaryless" or "paperless," which challenge individual business units to change their thinking, innovate, and develop or apply best practices in areas that are common to all businesses.

Former CEO Jack Welch coined the phrase "the boundaryless organization" to focus the company as a whole on breaking down the cultural, geographic, and organizational boundaries between employees. This encourages business units to think about their systems, skills, and organizational structure – themes that are relevant to all businesses in the group.

Workflow alignment

Organizations may also introduce major systems initiatives such as enterprise resource planning (ERP) or create common processes or information flows to promote alignment.

In manufacturing I used to be measured against manufacturing controlled costs – the biggest of which were labor and scrap. I could reduce scrap and optimize my labor costs by having very long production runs, but these would put pressure on purchasing and logistics by running down raw materials stocks and creating large inventories of finished goods.

I tried to improve the overall performance of the supply chain by reducing my production runs. I worked hard with the scheduling people to get that right and we saw quite significant improvements in raw materials and finished goods performance. Unfortunately, when it came to the end of the month the guys in raw materials claimed credit for their excellent purchasing performance, and the guys in finished goods told me what a good job they had done in improving warehouse utilization and distribution. Nobody would admit that it had anything to do with what I did and my numbers looked bad on their own.

My boss was unhappy, so the next month I turned the dial up. I made longer production runs than usual, my scrap went through the floor, I was a hero in my function, but suddenly everyone around me was complaining about this terrible manufacturing guy who was causing them supply and warehousing problems.

Eventually, I managed to get acceptance to look at the total picture, but I still spent the whole of the year looking bad on my financial measures because it was not possible to change those measures mid-year. Now that we have an enterprise-wide ERP system this is much easier. Everyone can see the impact of one part of the supply chain on the total picture.

Manufacturing director, FMCG, UK

Vertical and horizontal alignment

We can categorize the previous approaches as either "vertical" or "horizontal" alignment tools.

Vertical alignment is the top-down and bottom-up process of making sure that every individual understands their role in implementing the overall strategy of the business. It is also about ensuring that the learning from implementation is fed back to improve the strategy. Aligning around business strategy and the use of balanced scorecards are normally vertical alignment processes.

Horizontal alignment is the process of making sure that activities that cross vertical functions and geographies are aligned in the delivery of key processes and activities, such as serving global customers. Aligning around workflow, values and culture, and cross-business campaigns are all examples of horizontal alignment processes.

In a healthy matrix we need a balance of both horizontal and vertical alignment. We should recognize, however, that while each of these may be individually clear, collectively they may compete for our time and attention and may even conflict with each other.

This is a normal part of the "constructive tension" that is inherent in a matrix structure.

ALIGNING GOALS WITHIN YOUR OWN ROLE

At an individual level, we need tools for making visible any misalignment in goals between the different legs of our matrix and for understanding how to prioritize when resources are limited.

The alignment map helps individuals do this. You can define the arrows in any way that is meaningful to you; I have labeled them "vertical" and "horizontal." For you this could be business unit and function, or within a matrix role it could simply be the goals driven by manager A and the goals driven by manager B.

Use the tools provided in Chapters 3 and 4 to identify what is clear and what is not in both vertical and horizontal goal streams, and to seek out individuals who can help bring clarity to any areas that are not yet sufficiently defined.

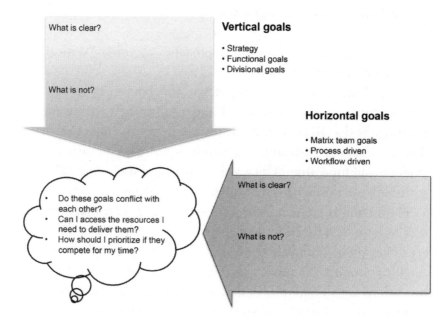

Figure 5.1 The alignment map

When we bring the streams together on the alignment map, there are three key questions that we need to answer.

Do these goals conflict with each other?

If goals from different legs of your matrix are in direct conflict or are inconsistent, then it will be impossible to meet them all.

If you have conflicting goals, you should organize a discussion with your horizontal and vertical managers to try to resolve them. You may find some of the tools in later chapters on managing dilemmas and tradeoffs useful in taking some options along to the meeting.

Can I access the resources I need to deliver these goals?

It is common for individuals, particularly those who are spread across multiple teams, to be given objectives that do not take into account the total range of their responsibilities.

Take the opportunity to review your total range of goals to see whether they are realistic within the timeframe and other resources you have available. You may not control all of the resources directly, but you do need to be able to gain access to them. If not, then you have to manage expectations among your stakeholders and managers.

Do this early in the goal-setting process, as later in the year it may simply look like complaining or justifying a potential failure.

How should I prioritize if these goals compete for my time?

Goals that compete for your time and attention are completely normal in a matrix (unless you have unlimited resources). You will regularly have to make choices about what to do first and what not to do at all.

This is nothing new; there were challenges over prioritization before the matrix. However, the matrix makes multiple perspectives part of the routine. Competing goals cannot be resolved merely by recourse to a single boss. Individuals need to be much more active in flagging up and reconciling prioritization challenges that may only be visible to them.

In the absence of clear criteria for prioritization, individuals in a matrix may prioritize on the basis of their own interests, the line of least resistance, or the most personal enjoyment.

Be explicit about the process you are using to prioritize, discuss it with your key stakeholders, and be clear about what you are doing in advance. Identify any knock-on effects of your decisions on others and let them know as soon as possible.

And be realistic. I very rarely meet anyone who feels they have all the resources they need to do their job; it is a matter of degree. In the competition for resources and attention, there will always be a tension between, for example, quality, time, and cost.

Resolving this is the job of management and cannot be driven out by even the most sophisticated process. If it was simple then we wouldn't need a manager; it would become a matter of routine administration.

If you are a manager in one leg of the matrix, you can help by making sure that you are aligned as far as possible with the other leg.

If managers are not aligned, then it is more difficult for individuals at the next level down to create alignment upward.

An aligned matrix is a little like a family. If a young child comes to Dad and asks "Can I go to my friend's house?" the first question Dad asks is "What did your mother say?" Parents naturally know that alignment is important; otherwise the kids drive a wedge between you and end up doing whatever they want.

This instinctive alignment, naturally checking in with what the other reporting line of the matrix is thinking, is far more powerful and effective than regular and detailed ARCI reviews or other formal processes.

MANAGING COMPETING PRIORITIES

The organizational alignment tools in this chapter can help in resolving competing priorities.

We have an overriding value of satisfying customer needs, but also some strong functional measures on operational efficiency.

We had a supply issue that was critical to customer satisfaction. The fastest way to solve it was one that reduced our manufacturing efficiency by creating more scrap. In our organization it is clear that the #1 priority is making sure that we do things right for the customer. However, we also know that any long-term solution needs to be efficient and reduce the cost of manufacturing too. This doesn't let me off the hook but it does help me make a decision – solve the customer problem first and then work on the efficiency problem.

Manufacturing director, food industry, China

However, competing priorities are one of the key reasons why we have a matrix; as I have already stressed, if we could decide on priorities once and for all, we would not need the matrix.

Competing priorities can exist for good reasons (different functional or role perspectives) or bad ones, such as accidentally misaligned objectives and power struggles. We need to ensure that our people have the skills, information, and confidence to manage this in our matrix; otherwise we will experience constant escalation to a higher level.

ALIGNING YOUR GOALS AND ROLE WITH OTHERS IN THE MATRIX

Once you are clear that your own goals are internally consistent, the next step is to make sure that your goals and role are aligned with the other individuals you work with regularly.

One simple but effective tool comes from a German matrix team training participant.

I have some permanent members on my team, but also some who are only dedicated between 10 percent and 50 percent to this team and one or two who are "on demand" and attend when needed.

We used to have a strong functional structure and this is the first time we have introduced the idea of the team goals driving functional activities. I was finding it hard to visualize all the goals and to get everyone aligned behind the overall team plan.

I created a large wall chart with the team goals along the left and columns for each of the functional representatives along the top. We used this to create a mapping of our goals and how they were aligned to the overall goals of the team.

It was a useful exercise: we found some gaps and overlaps and also some misunderstandings about priorities. It was also useful to find out about the goals that people had from other teams they were on and from their functions. We got a realistic understanding of how much time those individuals could spend on our team and what were their real priorities.

We will make this alignment exercise part of our planning process every year.

Brand team leader, healthcare, Germany

Matrix team alignment process

Matrix team goals	Function or individual #1	Function or individual #2	Function or individual #3
#1 team goal	My objectives and activities that support the delivery of this goal • • •		
#2 team goal	My objectives and activities that support the delivery of this goal • • •		
#3 team goal	My objectives and activities that support the delivery of this goal • • •		
Goals not aligned to this team	Other goals and activities that are from my function or other teams of which I am a member • • •		

1. The team or activity leader creates a grid, as here, and populates the left, shaded column with the key goals of the matrix team or project. Along the top are the names and functions of the other members of the team.

2. Underneath the list of team priorities, create space for individuals to record other goals and activities that are from their function or other teams.

3. Each individual on the team completes the boxes with their goals and activities that are aligned to and supporting each of the key matrix team goals. This clearly identifies any gaps or overlaps in support of the key goals of the virtual team. There will not necessarily be supporting activity from every function for every team goal.

4. The final row allows people to share activities and goals to which they are committed but that are not aligned to this particular virtual team. These are typically those activities in support of other teams or their functional goals.

5. Get each individual to present their column. From the content and style of their delivery, you will get an understanding of each individual's commitment and clarity around the team goals.

When you have completed this exercise, review the grid and discuss the following:

❏ **Gaps** – where necessary supporting goals from the functions are missing.

❏ **Overlaps** – where individuals are replicating work.

❏ **Misalignment** – where goals have mistakenly been included that do not match the team goals or priorities. Sometimes these will be misunderstandings or legacy activities from the old way of working that are no longer necessary.

❏ **Prioritization** – if individuals have large numbers of goals outside of those supporting this team, where does this team fit within their priorities?

❏ **Resourcing** – can you achieve these goals with the resources available?

I have found this to be a simple but useful tool for creating alignment. It can be created as a document and circulated to people in different locations, or it can be completed live with Post-it® notes as an alignment exercise in a goal-setting or kickoff meeting.

Goal overload

When you complete these exercises, you may find that you have too many goals. When we add an additional layer of reporting in a matrix, the risk is that we simply add more work.

It is unlikely that you will still be able to deliver all of the vertical responsibilities that you were able to complete before the matrix. After all, you have additional horizontal responsibilities for which you need to make room in your workload.

A question that companies rarely ask when introducing a matrix is: "What should the vertical stop doing in order to create space for the horizontal to succeed?"

Because you may be the only person who understands the full scope of your goals and role, you need to take personal responsibility for identifying and, if necessary, escalating any overload.

Most individuals do their best to cope, but some jobs are just not doable. It is not sustainable for individuals or organizations for these types of jobs to continue to exist.

Use the information in this chapter to ensure that the goals from the vertical and horizontal legs of your matrix are clearly aligned within your own role, that you have identified and dealt with conflicting priorities, and that your role is aligned with others around you.

Even after you use these alignment tools, you should expect still to experience competing goals and a certain level of dynamic tension between the different legs of the matrix. This is normal. In the next few chapters you will learn how to manage the tradeoffs, dilemmas, ambiguity, and even conflicts that are normal in matrix working.

Before you leave this chapter

❏ Are you clear about the high-level strategic goals of your organization, division, department, and team?

❏ Are you clear about the goals that are being driven by each leg of your matrix?

❏ If anything is not clear, how will you find out more details?

❏ Are the horizontal and vertical goals clear and sufficiently aligned within your role?

❏ Have you identified any competing priorities that are in direct conflict with each other? How will you resolve them?

❏ Are you clear about the goals and roles of others you work with regularly?

❏ Do your close colleagues understand your goals and role?

6

Difficult Decisions

Negotiations, choices, and tradeoffs

The test of a first-rate intelligence is the ability to hold two opposing ideas in mind at the same time and still retain the ability to function.
F Scott Fitzgerald

In Chapters 2 to 5 I have provided tools for clarifying and aligning goals, roles, and decision rights as far as possible. If we can bring clarity and alignment without undermining the flexibility we need in a matrix, then it makes sense to do so.

If we are able to give individuals the tools, skills, and confidence to take higher levels of ownership for their goals and roles and for aligning them with others, we will build higher levels of commitment and engagement.

However, the matrix is complex and ambiguous and we will inevitably face some difficult decisions when trying to resolve the competing demands and priorities of different legs of the matrix.

In this chapter I will introduce a framework for cutting through this complexity by thinking systematically about the choices available to us in resolving these competing demands. I will begin by looking at a model for framing the choices available and will then introduce some tools for managing complex tradeoffs, compromises, and sequences of choices. The chapter covers:

❑ The Five Choices framework
❑ The PickApart process – making your choices
❑ Quadrants 1 to 3 – tradeoffs, compromises, and sequences
❑ Quadrant 4 – deciding to do nothing

THE FIVE CHOICES FRAMEWORK

The tool I use to help people structure their thinking about choices and dilemmas is called the Five Choices framework. Global Integration developed it originally to help participants resolve cultural differences and find new ways of working together. We found that it was also a useful tool for helping people think through a whole range of dilemmas in matrix, virtual, and global working.

The framework is based on the understanding that, whenever we are looking at what appear to be two polar alternatives, we really have Five Choices in how we resolve them:

1. Choose option A.
2. Choose option B.
3. Compromise.
4. Choose to do nothing.
5. Find a higher-level combination of the options that satisfies both A and B.

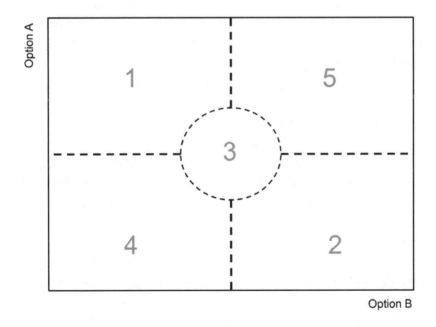

Figure 6.1   The Five Choices framework

We developed this tool to get people to think systematically about other alternatives to their own. In working across cultures, it is very common to begin by assuming that your own view is "correct." When you work internationally you soon realize that there are relatively few universals and many successful ways to get things done.

By systematically thinking through each of the five choices, we can defuse the trap of only considering our own cultural choice and we can increase creativity by identifying alternative ways of getting things done in different parts of the world.

Real-world problems, of course, are not as simple as consulting models. The resolution of complex challenges may include elements of each of these five choices. Let me give you an example.

I arrived at a conference in a rural area of Brazil to run a cross-cultural workshop for a global organization with headquarters in Switzerland but operating around the world. When I arrived on the second day of the meeting, it was not going well.

The hotel was operating on Bahia (Brazilian) time. It was very flexible with breaks and lunch at unpredictable times and it seemed impossible to get the hotel to change its way of working.

Latin American participants were used to moving around and answering the phone if it rang, so they were continually standing up, walking around, and leaving the room.

The Swiss senior managers were focused on timekeeping and the agenda and were frustrated with constant changes and what they saw as a lack of attention and discipline. They were concerned that this expensive meeting would not meet its objectives.

The meeting room looked out onto a beautiful beach where participants could watch the other hotel guests enjoying themselves and, just as the meeting was about to finish at around five o'clock, the sun would set. There was relatively little to do in the hotel in the evenings.

I explained the Five Choices framework to the participants and gave them the cross-cultural challenge of working out how to manage the remainder of the conference in a more positive way.

They decided that the fundamental underlying problem was different ideas about time and how it was organized (a common cross-cultural challenge). The Brazilian hotel had a very flexible view of time and the Swiss conference organizers had a very structured view of time.

Figure 6.2 is the solution they came up with. I have added the quadrant numbers in brackets to illustrate which of the five choices each decision represents. (In describing the model I use the term "quadrants," which of course refers to something divided into four. The correct word for something divided into five is a "quintant," but that word is obsolete and sounds cumbersome, so I hope you will forgive me if I continue to describe each of the five sections as a quadrant.)

We decided that we cannot change the hotel: we are only here for three days and they seem unable to change the way they work. We will adapt to them (Quadrant 2) when the coffee is served or the buffet is ready on the plates, then we will take a break – whenever that is.

It is also normal that people in Latin America respond immediately to urgent calls and so we should expect a certain amount of this to go on. Participants and the organizers have agreed that they will start the meeting when 80 percent of people are back following breaks, but will stop the meeting if we fall below 80 percent of participants in the room (Quadrant 3 – a compromise, not everyone was happy with this but they decided they could live with it).

We are frustrated watching people enjoying the beach and then having little to do in the evening, so we suggest that after lunch is served (whenever that is) we take a three-hour break so people can enjoy the beach and other facilities (Quadrant 5 – everyone liked this one).

But we also accept that this is an expensive conference and it is important to finish the agenda and achieve the objectives. When we get back from lunch, we will continue working in the evening until we have completed the agenda for the day – however long that takes (Quadrant 1).

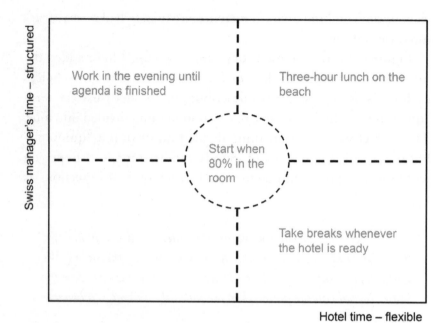

Figure 6.2 The Five Choices framework – Brazilian conference

As a solution this worked well and, because the group came up with the ideas themselves, they implemented the new rules enthusiastically.

We can apply this kind of thinking to the choices and dilemmas we face within a matrix. The rest of this chapter will provide examples of when we should prefer each of these choices and will demonstrate how we move around Quadrants 1 to 4 to find the right solution to our particular problems.

Chapter 7 will focus on how to find the right approach to the most challenging dilemmas by getting to Quadrant 5.

THE PICKAPART PROCESS – MAKING YOUR CHOICES

If the Five Choices framework is the tool, then PickApart is the process we use to help people think about which is the right choice for them in a specific situation.

For a given business area or topic, we do the following:

❏ Identify the central dilemma we are trying to solve.

❏ Break down the specific elements or activities that need to be delivered in this area.

❏ Make conscious decisions on which quadrant describes how we will deliver each of these.

A learning and development organization (L&D) was being challenged to work more globally. The dilemma it was facing was what should be global and what should remain local within the function. Global Integration brought together some of the key stakeholders and led them through the PickApart process, as follows.

We asked participants to identify on Post-it notes all the activities that the L&D function carried out. We then asked them to discuss and agree in which of the five quadrants each of these activities should be placed.

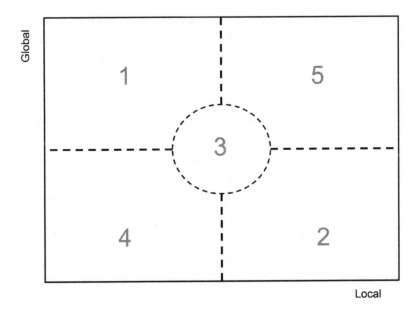

Figure 6.3 The PickApart process

Some decisions were straightforward:

❏ There should be a global L&D system to give information on what training has been delivered – Quadrant 1.
❏ There should be some common competencies for people in global leadership positions – Quadrant 1.
❏ For some core corporate programs the organization wanted the same message delivered everywhere in the world, such as corporate values and business ethics – Quadrant 1.
❏ Programs like basic presentation skills or meetings skills training were available in most countries and in local languages, so there was little value to be gained in standardizing them – Quadrant 2.

Some questions, however, were less simple. Should leadership training be global or local? The organization found it hard to place a Post-it note labeled "leadership training" on the framework.

In operating this process, if the question is difficult to answer, it probably means that you are asking it at too high a level. The answer is to go down to a greater level of detail. So we "picked apart" the issue of leadership training in more detail and matters became clearer:

❏ First-line supervisory training would be delivered locally and in the local language – Quadrant 2.
❏ Leaders above a certain grade and high potentials would be expected to attend a global program at HQ; part of the objective was to help them build their global network, so this would be a common worldwide initiative – Quadrant 1.
❏ Junior and middle managers would attend programs run on a regional basis to reflect differences in leadership styles in Asia, Europe, and the Americas – Quadrant 5; everyone felt this was a good solution.

The value of a process like this is in the conversations it provokes and the development of agreement among stakeholders.

Most issues fall naturally into one of the quadrants. More complex or multidimensional issues can be resolved by picking apart the topic into greater levels of detail.

Using the Five Choices framework in negotiation

In resolving dilemmas or disagreements between two individual points of view, we can use the Five Choices framework to structure our alternatives.

A global marketing director, speaking with his country marketing head, discussed the organization of marketing activities worldwide. The global marketing director had some "my way" (Quadrant 1) issues. In these areas he insisted on one common way of working and he had the power to make sure that this was implemented.

They were also able to have a discussion about things that were naturally local or "your way" – Quadrant 2. Anything that was heavily influenced by local legislation, regulation, or strong consumer preferences had to be compliant with local needs.

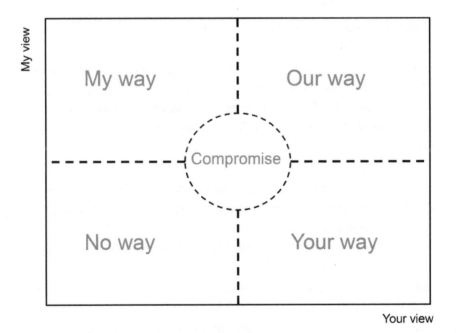

Figure 6.4 Structuring alternatives

There were also a number of local market activities such as sponsorship, where having a global input added very little value. It was important to recognize this, as the country marketing people felt as though everything was being taken over at the global level. Recognizing the logically local activities defused much of the concern about losing autonomy over marketing decisions.

There was a much longer discussion around an upcoming major sporting event, which was being held locally but was part of a global television and marketing campaign. Here they needed Quadrant 5 ("our way") solutions, because the event would be visible internationally.

This can be a useful framework for resolving disagreements between two legs of the matrix on goals and priorities.

QUADRANTS 1 TO 3 – TRADEOFFS, CONSTRAINTS, SEQUENCES, AND COMPROMISES

Tradeoffs and constraints

A tradeoff is a situation that involves losing some element of something in return for gaining another element of something else.

In a tradeoff, the two factors are usually mutually exclusive; for example, I can have a higher-quality product if I spend more money.

> *A decision without tradeoffs ... isn't a decision. The art of good decision making is looking forward to and celebrating the tradeoffs, not pretending they do not exist.*
>
> Seth Godin, US entrepreneur and author

The need for a tradeoff implies constraint. There must be a limitation in resources, such as time or finance, which means that we cannot have all of what we want, and that forces us to choose.

The management of tradeoffs requires a thorough understanding of the upsides and downsides of each choice. There is always a cost involved, even if it is only an opportunity cost. In acquiring more of A, I cannot acquire as much of B.

What is the tradeoff you face?

Questions	Factor #1	Factor #2
What are the positives of choosing this factor at the expense of the other?		
What are your concerns in only choosing this at the expense of the other factor?		
What is the minimum acceptable level of this factor that you must achieve?		
What are the constraints that make this a tradeoff?		
What can you live with?		

In our projects we often face a tradeoff between cost and speed. We can deliver projects faster, but it typically costs more as we need to apply more resources. Managing this tradeoff is the story of my life.
Project manager, engineering, Argentina

Nevertheless, tradeoffs do not have to be binary choices. For example, we can present a range of values for the tradeoff between cost and speed. It does not have to be 100 percent of one or 100 percent of the other.

In evaluating pros and cons it is important to be as fact based as possible – to take into account real costs and other objective measures. There may be intangible or emotional costs involved in making a choice, which should also be considered.

I can delay delivering my project plan in order to attend this customer meeting. I think it is the right thing to do, but it will make me look bad with my project manager and he's been really helpful to me this year.

Virtual team member, healthcare, Malaysia

It may be possible to define minimum acceptable standards and to make sure that, in finding the right tradeoff, we continue to have some flexibility.

In managing tradeoffs, by definition, we usually end up not getting 100 percent of what we want. Tradeoffs are rarely perfect and the key question we should ask when we reach a potential tradeoff is: "Can we live with it?"

Because tradeoffs are defined by the constraint that stops you from having both, for example limits to budget or time, then if we can remove or change the constraint, we can sometimes remove the need for tradeoffs.

In his "theory of constraints," Eliyahum M Goldratt develops the theme that the chain is only as strong as its weakest link. He demonstrates that in many cases processes are vulnerable because the weakest person or part of the process can break or delay progress. The theory of constraints has mainly been applied to supply-chain issues in order to identify bottlenecks and constraints and remove them to increase the capability of the whole process.

I used the theory of constraints in my manufacturing days to change the way we dealt with a major constraint to production capacity: changeover time.

It used to take up to four hours to change one of our production lines to cope with different types of drinks ingredients and packaging. I read that Toyota had found a way to change the massive dies that press car bodies in one minute, so I challenged our production engineers to make a radical reduction in the time it took to change our line.

They returned with a solution that cut the changeover to two hours. I told them that Toyota could do it in one minute and asked them to think again. After visiting Toyota, they came back and told me that the auto company was "cheating." It didn't change the die quickly at all; it simply slid it out of the production line, slotted in a new die, and then had all the time in the world to do the changeover of the original machine, which was no longer holding up production.

I asked if we could cheat too and they came up with the same solution: a set of change parts that could be taken out as a module, replaced, and cleaned offline. This reduced changeover times from four hours to a few minutes.

I used to have to take changeover times into account in managing the tradeoff between production run length and inventory. Losing four hours of production meant that I would prefer longer production runs, even if it built higher levels of stock. By effectively removing this constraint, I no longer had to pay attention to this tradeoff.

❏ What are the constraints that are causing you to have to make tradeoff decisions?
❏ Can you eliminate or reduce the constraint to a level at which you no longer need to worry about the tradeoff?

Sometimes by defining the constraints and limits of an area of responsibility clearly, we can give people more freedom to operate within or around them.

Sequence of choices

A number of apparently polar opposites can be resolved by dealing with both in sequence, rather than trying to achieve a constant state of balance. Remember our example from Chapter 5.

We have an overriding value of satisfying customer needs, but also some strong functional measures on operational efficiency.

We had a supply issue that was critical to customer satisfaction. The fastest way to solve it was one that reduced our manufacturing efficiency by creating more scrap. In our organization it is clear that the #1 priority is making sure that we do things right for the customer. However, we also know that any long-term solution needs to be efficient and reduce the cost of manufacturing too.

This doesn't let me off the hook, but it does help me make a decision – solve the customer problem first and then work on the efficiency problem.

Manufacturing director, food industry, China

This organization's values and priorities helped simplify the decision about what to do. First choose Quadrant 1 – satisfy the customer – then move to Quadrant 2 and fix the efficiency issue.

Compromises

If we could add a scale to our Five Choices framework with 0–10 on each axis, then a compromise would be a 5:5 solution. A compromise is where we agree to meet in the middle; each of us agrees to give up something in order to reach agreement.

We spent 12 months trying to agree on a common pay-for-performance framework for our global business. In the end, after many meetings and discussions, we came up with a form of words that everyone could agree with. The words left the definitions of both pay and performance quite vague, so in reality it allowed each of us to continue doing what we currently do. We compromised to get agreement, but what was the point in the discussion if we all carry on doing what we always did?

HR manager, business services, Russia

Compromises can also emerge when one individual gives up because the issue is simply not important enough for them to continue fighting. This is rarely a basis for a good decision and may merely provide a way out of making the necessary decisions.

In general, if you are coming up with several Quadrant 3 solutions, make sure that these are really moving you forward and not just establishing the lowest common denominator as the new norm.

Sometimes going down to a lower level of detail with the PickApart process can help open up the debate toward a more positive conclusion.

QUADRANT 4 – DECIDING TO DO NOTHING

Although participants on our training programs rarely come up with a "do nothing" solution to dilemmas, this is often what we do in real life. Dilemmas are difficult and we can usually see the benefits of both sides of the argument. If we consider that these dilemmas cannot be resolved, sometimes we just walk away from them.

There are many occasions in management where "do nothing for a while and see what happens" can be a successful strategy. Many problems solve themselves; some interpersonal challenges go away if given time, when a confrontation may have made them worse. However, when we are talking about deeply rooted dilemmas, these are unlikely to resolve themselves.

A decision not to do anything means that the situation will probably remain unchanged. Be aware, however, that Quadrant 4 is a choice – you are *choosing* the status quo.

Use the information in this chapter to structure your thinking about the dilemmas you face in your matrix. Think about elements of a solution that could fall into each of the five quadrants and use the framework systematically for managing tradeoffs, choices, and compromises.

In the next chapter we will look at how to solve true dilemmas to get to Quadrant 5.

Before leaving this chapter

❑ What are the key dilemmas that you face?

❑ What are the key underlying choices that you are being asked to make?

❑ Can you pick the issue apart into elements that fall naturally into each of the five quadrants?

❑ Have you identified the pros and cons for your major tradeoffs?

❑ Can you change the constraints that are forcing you to make tradeoffs?

❑ Can you resolve these choices by being clear about the sequence of actions?

❑ Are you settling for too many compromises?

❑ Where have you decided to do nothing?

7

Dealing with Daily Dilemmas

Dilemmas, polarities, and learning journeys

In the last chapter we looked at decisions requiring choices between two alternatives or tradeoffs. However, true dilemmas arise when we cannot easily choose between A and B – we need both.

We set up a matrix because we need to be good at managing dilemmas. To succeed, we need both the global and the local, the product group and the function, the horizontal and the vertical.

In this chapter I will look at how to get to Quadrant 5 in the Five Choices framework. I will introduce two processes for developing true win–win solutions and consider how we can use them to resolve the daily dilemmas that are normal in a matrix. The chapter covers:

❑ Getting to Quadrant 5
❑ Is it a real dilemma? Positions, interests, and framing
❑ Managing polarities
❑ The learning journey
❑ It is a judgment call

It is not possible or even desirable to resolve dilemmas once and for all – we cannot usually choose the global and ignore the local, for example. Instead, we have to develop the skills to manage these dilemmas by making sophisticated choices and developing more creative solutions that enable us either to do both, or at least to find the right balance for that moment, with an understanding that the correct balance tomorrow may be different.

GETTING TO QUADRANT 5

If a compromise is a 5:5 solution, then Quadrant 5 represents a solution where each party gets more than 5.

I have had long discussions with engineers and mathematicians about whether a 10:10 solution is really achievable – where each side gains 100 percent of what they are looking for. I would still like to think that we can in theory, but realistically most Quadrant 5 solutions are somewhere in the 6:6 to 9:9 range.

Writers and politicians glibly talk about synergies, the "third way," and "glocal" solutions to problems. Usually they offer few ideas on how to actually get to that kind of solution. They tell us that "it works better for both of us" or "it feels fair to everyone involved."

The questions that busy managers with real problems ask me are: "How do I create these solutions?" and "I understand it is a good idea in principle, but how do I do it in practice?" The challenge is to come up with some systematic tools that help us get to where we want, instead of optimistic platitudes.

First, we should recognize that it is usually easier to deal with choices and tradeoffs. As we have seen with the PickApart process in Chapter 6, if we find the right level of understanding and granularity to discuss issues, we can often make the choices much clearer.

However, when PickApart identifies issues that are important enough to require a Quadrant 5 solution, we need a process and the willingness and creativity to move beyond our historical ideas and create something new. Three approaches may help: positions, interests, and reframing.

IS IT A REAL DILEMMA? POSITIONS, INTERESTS, AND REFRAMING

In negotiation theory, we learn to distinguish between:

❏ Positions – what people want from the negotiation, often without disclosing their underlying motive.
❏ Interests – why they want that.

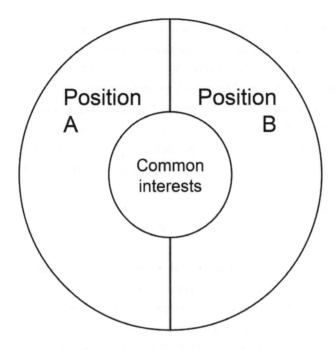

Figure 7.1 Common interests

It is often easier to find a resolution by understanding each other's underlying interests and looking for creative ways to satisfy them both, rather than simply stating positions and demands and falling into the process of compromise and negotiation.

In developing Quadrant 5 solutions, it is always useful to get people to understand *why* they want the things they want.

By focusing on meeting these underlying interests and needs, we can often take what appears to be a dilemma and defuse it. Interests may be shared and compatible even when positions are different.

A process engineering manager and a production supervisor were fighting over access to a production line. The production supervisor needed the line to run some product to hit the production schedule, while the process engineering manager wanted to run some trials to improve the running of the machine. It descended into a battle for access between two functions, manufacturing and R&D.

When we pushed to understand their underlying interests in more detail, it turned out that the R&D trial was designed to increase the speed of the production line and that they needed some product to run through the process to make sure it was working effectively. The production supervisor was keen to see an improvement in the speed of the process and was prepared to take a small risk with the higher levels of scrap the trial would entail in order to support the development. A solution based on these common interests was easy to find.

Production director, FMCG, Brazil

Reconciling on the basis of shared interests usually leads to stronger and more mutual solutions, rather than compromises that may fall apart in the future. Finding solutions like this requires consideration of the other person's position and underlying interests, as well as an open dialogue with a genuine desire to find a resolution.

This approach will not work with issues of resource allocation where resource either has to go to A or to B (and there is no creative solution to remove or get around the constraint) – these are tradeoffs and should be managed as such. It also is unlikely to help when the disputes are about fundamental values differences. These are likely to be deeply rooted and resistant to change.

Here is a process for uncovering interests:

❏ **Define the problem.** Be clear about what the issue or problem is. Write it down and agree that this is the real issue at stake.

❏ **Understand the background to the problem and any barriers to resolution.** Identify the specific things that are impeding progress.

❏ **Depersonalize it.** Try to keep the issues objective. We need to recognize that emotions and individual feelings often influence our interests as well as our positions, but try to stop the discussion from becoming emotional. Focus on the specific challenges to be resolved.

❏ **Identify the underlying interests.** Why does each party want the things they do? These could be tangible deliverables or could be less tangible issues of trust or confidence. Look for common ground and shared interests.

❏ Build on these previous stages to look for creative solutions that meet as many of the interests as possible.

Reframing

Sometimes we cannot change the world, but we can change the way we feel about it by reframing what we observe.

When we receive a complaint about a service or our way of working, we can see this as a challenge to our capability or professionalism, or we can view it as a suggestion for how to improve.

If our initial response to a suggestion or idea is negative, or if we immediately become defensive or feel the need to justify our actions, then we should stop and try to reframe it – look for the positive intent behind it. The issue may not be a dilemma or a tradeoff, but in fact an opportunity.

I was waiting for an important meeting with an Arab client. I was aware that norms on punctuality are different in their culture than in my own (I am always obsessively on time) and came prepared to wait with plenty of time for my meeting. I congratulated myself on my cultural planning when 15 minutes after the scheduled start of the meeting I was still sitting in the waiting area.

After 30 minutes I kept reminding myself that this was not unusual, but I couldn't help feeling frustrated. In my culture punctuality is a sign of respect and when we keep people waiting, it is usually because we are playing power games.

I thought more about what I knew about this Arab culture. Relationships were incredibly important, but it was quite hard to meet people if you were from outside the culture. I realized that I was sitting in the waiting room of a high-status Arab manager and missing an opportunity to meet other people who were waiting around me.

I started to make conversation with other people in the area, a couple exchanged business cards, and we had some fascinating discussions about cultural differences. By the time I was called into my contact's office, I was feeling a little disappointed not to have more time to meet people.

I realized that I couldn't change the punctuality habits of a whole country just because I was visiting, but I could change how I felt about it.

Sales director, construction, Switzerland

Positions, interests, and reframing are simple processes. Nothing works in all cases, but trying these will at least help you have a thorough exploration of your own and others' motivations and interests behind an issue, before you conclude that it is a real dilemma.

If it turns out that you do have a real dilemma, then the next two tools may help.

MANAGING POLARITIES

In his book *Polarity Management*, Barry Johnson defines polarities as "sets of opposites which cannot function well independently. Because the two sides of a polarity are interdependent, you cannot choose one as a 'solution' and neglect the other. The objective of the polarity management perspective® is to get the best of both opposites, while avoiding the limits of each."

He goes on to describe the typical journeys between the two poles of a polarity in a number of contexts.

One example of applying this thinking to a matrix dilemma would be the advantages and disadvantages of a functional structure or a more flexible matrix.

In traditional organizations in the past we have focused on a clear functional structure, which had some advantages:

❏ Accountabilities and authority were clear.
❏ People had control over their resources.
❏ Functional decision making was fast.
❏ Bureaucracy was limited.
❏ Goals and roles were simpler.

Unfortunately, there is no such thing as a free lunch; there is always a downside, a set of disadvantages, to any approach. The disadvantages of a functional structure include:

❑ Resources were locked up in silos.
❑ Cooperation and communication across silos were difficult.
❑ Cross-functional decision making was slow.
❑ Global and regional activities received lower priority.
❑ People had narrower perspectives.
❑ Needs of global or regional customers were not well met.

Unsurprisingly, these disadvantages create energy for change. These are the typical problems that cause companies to consider a more flexible organizational structure such as a matrix.

So we start to seek out the advantages of the opposite pole – the matrix. The advantages of a matrix include:

❑ Improved access to shared resources.
❑ Improved cooperation and communication across silos.
❑ Flexibility through faster decisions.
❑ Improved global and regional projects, systems, and customer service.
❑ Broader people development.

In the search for organizational flexibility we may choose to adopt matrix working, or even a formal matrix structure. However, if we do not manage the matrix effectively, we may find that we experience the disadvantages of this more flexible approach, including:

❑ Unclear accountabilities.
❑ Slow decision making.
❑ Bureaucracy and too many meetings.
❑ Increased conflict over resources.
❑ Higher levels of uncertainty.

If we experience these downsides this creates a counter force, a demand to move back to a simpler and more structured functional way of working – and we are back where we started!

This can create what Johnson calls an "infinity loop," where we cycle away from problems toward the solutions of the opposite pole, but if we focus too much on this new pole, we experience the disadvantages of that approach and this creates a demand to cycle back in search of the advantages of the previous pole, and so the infinity loop continues (the looping central arrow on Figure 7.2).

This may help explain why organizations cycle between more structured and more flexible ways of operating, with each direction seeming to bring benefits, but over time causing problems, leading us to cycle back to the other pole.

The way to break out of this loop is to focus on achieving the advantages while at the same time making sure that we do not focus too strongly on that pole, thereby causing the disadvantages and the counter force against what we are trying to achieve.

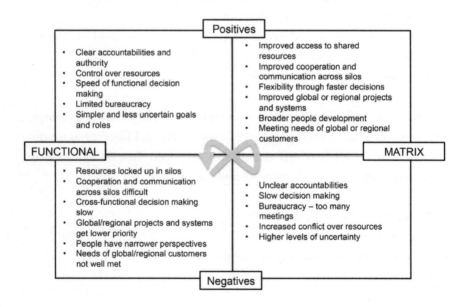

Figure 7.2 Summary of the matrix/functional journey

In introducing a matrix organization, we are trying to attain the positives of the top-right quadrant. At the same time, we want to avoid the negatives of the bottom-right quadrant. We need to be alert to these potential negatives, and prevent them by giving people the skills and capabilities to create the right level of clarity on structure, even within the matrix.

We observe that many organizations prefer to focus on process: creating more guidelines, process maps, and role descriptions in an attempt to cope with ambiguity. If process is not balanced with the development of new skills and ways of working, it may lead back to focusing too much on structure.

You can use the polarity management approach to structure your thinking about any matrix or other challenge that has two distinct poles, for instance:

❏ The global and local.
❏ The generalist and the specialist.
❏ Control and trust.
❏ Clarity and ambiguity.

A polarity is not a problem to be solved once and for all; the two poles are interdependent. We cannot have 100 percent flexibility and 0 percent structure. Polarities need continuous management. Therefore, we need to develop the capability and tools to manage these challenges, which are normal in a matrix.

In addition to Barry Johnson's book, *Polarity Coaching* by Kathy Anderson applies the techniques to some typical coaching topics.

THE LEARNING JOURNEY

It is rare that an organization jumps straight to the final form of a complex organizational structure. There is more likely to be a journey of exploration and learning, with a number of phases that lead to an organizational form that works.

In resolving real dilemmas, it is unusual to experience the "one bound and we are free" moment when everything falls into place and all problems are solved. In fact, we should distrust any "magic bullet" solution from consultants or authors, on the basis that real life is complicated. We have to put some work, intelligence, and creativity into applying these tools to our own particular business challenges, culture, and environment.

We should expect the journey toward resolving a major dilemma to take time and to suffer some reverses and false starts before we find a solution that really works.

I call this the learning journey and it has a number of predictable phases and elements:

❏ The learning journey usually starts in either Quadrant 1 or 2 of the Five Choices framework. The early phases are similar to those described in the section on polarity management – we have taken advantage of the functional structure, for example, but we are starting to see the downside in a lack of flexibility. If we are centralized we have seen some efficiencies, but we have begun to realize that we lack responsiveness to local competition.

❏ When enough people in the organization at senior levels are dissatisfied with this, it creates the energy and counter force that make the opposite quadrant seem more attractive – "the grass is always greener on the other side."

❏ The organization begins the journey toward the opposite quadrant. If we were centralized before, now we move to greater decentralization and we reap the benefits. However, we start to realize that there are some downsides to this approach.

❏ Typically, the learning journey continues in the new direction until a critical mass of influential people in the organization think "this has gone too far." This creates the energy for the counter swing.

❏ In the learning journey we do not just cycle around the "infinity loop," we try to break out of it to create a virtuous spiral, where we preserve the benefits that we have gained from the previous leg of the journey and only move back in the other direction selectively in specific areas, to try to recapture the benefits we lost when we moved away from our previous position.

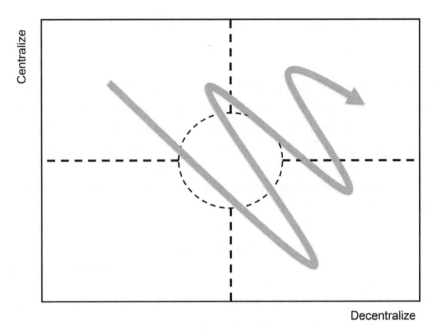

Figure 7.3 The learning journey

❏ We lock in the elements of the culture and way of operating that run best in the new decentralized manner.
❏ We identify the specific disadvantages we are experiencing in the new way of working and start to experiment with new ways of organizing those elements.

This process is a subjective one. The journey that an organization takes is largely driven by the opinions of the people within it, and these are shaped by personality, culture, and history. For example:

❏ A highly centralized global brands company decentralized decision making in advertising for the first time to Europe. The US HQ did not feel that the first European adverts really reflected the essence of the brand. Senior leaders were uncomfortable (many of them had resisted the change in the first place) and advertising responsibility was quickly returned to the USA.
❏ A highly decentralized Danish pharmaceutical company introduced a common financial control system for the first time.

Powerful country managers resisted this "Stalinist" control mechanism.

Corporate culture shapes the learning journey in many ways. The most powerful is by influencing people's perceptions of change. If we are accustomed to high levels of control, then even a little decentralization feels risky. If complete autonomy is the norm, then the slightest request for information or control can seem like a power grab.

Leaders who initiate change and then adapt and alter direction are sometimes accused of making a U-turn.

You turn if you want to; the lady's not for turning.

Margaret Thatcher

A politician who changes his or her mind, realizes that an initiative is not working, and reverses it is accused of making a "U-turn" and is immediately put under pressure to resign.

In business we call this learning and it is essential! If you never change your mind, you never learn anything. The challenge is to keep learning and creating higher-order solutions rather than merely repeating the failed journeys of the past.

U-turns are a normal part of the learning journey, provided that we do not abandon the learning and benefits from the first part of the journey, but instead find ways to build on them.

A fast-food restaurant operator exported its US product menu around the world. Many of the items were well accepted and the business started to grow. However, it started to get feedback that consumers in some countries preferred other products that weren't on the menu. Initially it resisted this, as the existing US formula seemed to be working well overall (Quadrant 1).

Then it began to expand into markets that were very different culturally. In India, Hindus would not eat beef burgers; many Indians are vegetarian. The fast-food restaurant had never offered a vegetarian option but, because of the size of the market, it felt it had to (Quadrant 2).

It also developed products to compete with local favorites like pizza in Italy and chicken tikka masala in the UK.

Then it started to realize that this product innovation was quite useful in other markets. There was a substantial vegetarian market around the world that it currently was not satisfying, so it took these products and offered them in more places.

The company found that some initiatives were truly global – it linked the rollout of products and marketing campaigns to major Hollywood movies that were shown around the world.

It also discovered that some activities were purely local. It was forced into offering beer in Germany because local customers demanded it, but chose not to extend this to other markets, as it felt uncomfortable with alcoholic beverages as part of its product line.

Enormous benefits were gained by applying the learning from the global supply chain to developing local suppliers of key ingredients. The company has single-handedly increased the capability for food production in some regions.

As we move toward the top-right quadrant, we need to be increasingly creative. The question then becomes how we can get increased levels of one through the other, rather than choosing between them.

❑ How can we become more global through serving our customers locally in a way that makes us more effective globally?

We do not call it a headquarters, we call it a "store service center"; the words are important. Instead of being seen as the source of power and direction, we have an obsessive focus on what works locally. Most innovation and new ideas come from people who are close to the customer. Our job is to find out what works and spread it, to take innovation and offer it to more markets, not to kill it through a weight of process and central bureaucracy. This focus on the local gives us more options to compete with globally.

Operations manager, retail, UK

❑ How can we centralize in a way that allows us to be more flexible and get the benefits of decentralization?

We centralized our information systems so that we could get common data flows, definitions, and the ability to consolidate our numbers on a global basis. However, the real benefit of having this information was that we were able to make it available much faster and in a much more useful form to people in our local operations. We used it to decentralize decision making. If we used the central systems to centralize decision making too then that would have slowed us down.

IT director, engineering, Japan

For more examples of developing creative solutions to management dilemmas, read Charles Hampden-Turner's *Charting the Corporate Mind*.

IT IS A JUDGMENT CALL

Managing dilemmas is often a matter of judgment, which is a challenging skill to develop.

Good judgment comes from experience. Experience comes from bad judgment.

Rita Mae Brown

To develop judgment we need the opportunity to make repeated decisions and get feedback on whether they were successful or not.

We employ seismologists to run surveys and decide whether there is likely to be oil in a particular location. They make the decision on whether to sink a test well. This is a big decision costing many millions of dollars, so we need to get it right. Seismologists get to make a decision on whether they think we should drill about six or seven times in a typical career. A big problem is that young seismologists are considerably more optimistic than old seismologists!

To try to improve their judgment, we organized a training course. On the first morning they were given the readings, reports, core samples, and other data from a real survey and at the end of the morning they were asked to decide – should we drill?

As soon as they made the decision, the actual seismologists who had been involved in the real case came through the door and told them what actually happened. They got real-time feedback on the accuracy of their judgment.

In the afternoon, we did the same thing again. By the end of the week they had had ten opportunities to exercise judgment in real cases and receive feedback. This compressed the decisions of a whole career into one week. By the end of the week, their judgment calls were considerably more accurate.

Operations director, oil exploration, Mexico

In our training on corporate values, we present the values and principles that we try to operate under and then we give participants some mini-cases, based on real situations.

It is easy to say that quality, efficiency, or integrity are important – the real challenge is where we have to make some judgment calls. Do we compromise efficiency for quality? Where is the line on integrity when working in countries with different laws and traditions?

We ask new associates to use the values and principles of the business to come up with what they think are the right solutions. We then get them to discuss their judgments with experienced managers who have been involved in similar situations to get feedback on what the organization would actually do. These are usually excellent discussions and really bring the values of the business to life.

Talent manager, chemicals, China

You can improve people's ability to make judgment calls through simulation and feedback.

Use the following process to drive a discussion on how you want people to reconcile tradeoffs and dilemmas in your organization:

❏ Create some examples that are relevant to your industry and business.
❏ Get individuals to discuss them and propose solutions.

❏ Give the individuals feedback from experienced managers, who discuss the judgments they made to help them calibrate and improve their judgment in these complex areas.

Use the information in this chapter to identify and start to resolve some of the key dilemmas that you face in your matrix. Make sure that your people have the capabilities to find the right balance for your business.

Before you leave this chapter

❏ What are the key dilemmas that you face?
❏ Are they real dilemmas or simply difference in interests and positions?
❏ Can you create a polarity map that describes the situation?
❏ Where are you in the learning journey? What are your next steps?
❏ Do your people have the skills and judgment to be able to resolve dilemmas in the matrix?

8

Creating and
Coping with Conflict

What to do when nothing
else works

The matrix is complex: we experience competing goals, we need to cooperate with diverse groups of colleagues from different cultures and functions, and we have to manage tradeoffs and dilemmas. This complexity can lead to higher levels of disagreement and conflict.

Conflict occurs when one party wants to impose their views on the other, despite their needs or feelings. It tends to become emotional, personal, and entrenched. Conflict is often more about style than content.

When one individual tries to impose their views on another, it will frequently create anger and resistance. This damages the positive working relationships that are essential to good employee engagement and productivity.

In this chapter I will outline some particular challenges in identifying and managing conflict in matrix organizations. The chapter covers:

❏ How do we storm remotely?
❏ The conflict sequence – managing the process
❏ The five conflict modes

Conflict is only constructive if afterward the relationship is improved, people have a better understanding of each other's needs and interests, and the conflict doesn't reoccur.

Just talking about things, venting, or letting off steam may feel good at the time, but if it does not solve the problem, then the conflict is likely to crop up again in the future. And because we have relatively little face-to-face time in many matrix teams, we need to have the skills to recognize and deal with conflicts quickly.

Conflict can occur in any organization, but in a matrix we have some particular challenges:

❏ The nature of dual reporting lines means that we will naturally have competing goals and overlapping accountabilities.
❏ Resources are limited and shared more widely across the organization, so resource allocation can provoke a heated debate.
❏ Priorities will always be a challenge and will change constantly.
❏ Teams will include a more diverse group of colleagues from different functions and cultures. The more perspectives we bring to bear, the more opportunities for misunderstanding and different views there will be.
❏ The opportunities for misunderstanding messages through email and other media is often higher than in face-to-face communication.

The conflict management literature tends to divide the types of conflict at work into two types:

❏ **Warranted conflict** – sincere disagreements about goals and outcomes.
❏ **Unwarranted conflict** – where goals are accepted but there is disagreement about how they should be achieved. This form of conflict often involves style and behavior differences or misinterpretations and is much more common.

Warranted conflict can usually be resolved by using the tools from Chapters 3 to 5 to achieve goal and role clarity and alignment. In this chapter I will focus on resolving unwarranted conflicts.

We will look at a very simple model of managing conflict in matrix teams, followed by a more detailed conflict-management sequence that can be followed when resolving conflicts in our own team or organization.

HOW DO WE STORM REMOTELY?

One of the simplest models of team development was proposed by Bruce Tuckman in 1965. He said that teams go through four phases, each of which needs to be resolved before we achieve high performance.

The phases are as follows:

❏ **Form** – we create a team and people start to work together and find out about each other.
❏ **Storm** – individuals share their different ideas and perspectives and there may be disagreements on goals, ways of working, and so on. This might be quite a mild process or it could lead to major disagreements based around misunderstandings or unresolved issues.
❏ **Norm** – we develop agreed ways of working and shared values; team members buy into these collectively.
❏ **Perform** – only when we have resolved each of the previous stages can we really become a high-performing team.

The big challenge in distributed teams is: "When do we get to storm?" We need the skills to create opportunities for conflict to arise and be resolved effectively.

> *I work in a team where there are quite a lot of disagreements that never get resolved. We do not meet face to face, so when a disagreement occurs repeatedly it is tempting just to put the call on hold and ignore it.*
>
> Customer services associate, insurance, USA

It is essential that we enable the storming and norming phases of the process to happen close together. If all we do is storm, we may feel better for a while but nothing gets resolved. Once the issues have been "stormed," it is important to make the time to develop new norms, new ways of working, that prevent these problems from happening again in the future.

To promote storming and norming, some of my clients hold specific events designed to allow this to happen quickly in a managed, usually face-to-face environment.

We call them "drains up" meetings. When two departments or teams have problems working together, we bring them together in a workshop. We get them to identify all of the issues and concerns and explore them from both perspectives. The purpose of the workshop is to put actions in place to make sure we resolve the differences and work together better in the future.

Network manager, telecoms, Canada

Inexperienced leaders or individuals who are conflict averse may try to suppress the storming phase, as it can feel risky and unpleasant. However, if storming does not happen and new norms are not developed, the team will get stuck at the storming phase: conflicts will not be resolved and will reoccur. It is important to let each of these phases happen.

Individuals from cultures where group harmony is important may be deeply uncomfortable with an open storming phase. In cross-cultural teams it may be necessary to have one-on-one discussions with individuals, rather than making storming a collective process.

THE CONFLICT SEQUENCE –
MANAGING THE PROCESS

A simple but effective sequence for managing conflict has four stages:

1. Recognize and flag the problem.
2. Understand the differences.
3. Create shared purpose.
4. Build and deliver agreement.

I will outline some of the key principles in managing each stage of the conflict sequence from the perspective of an individual who is directly involved in the conflict. If you are a manager or mediator,

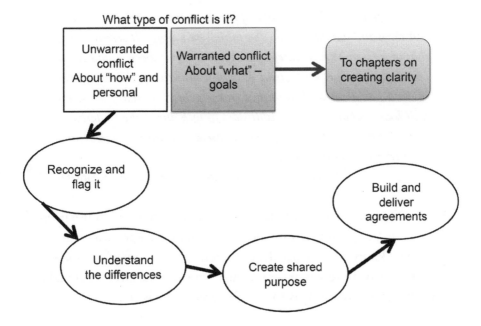

Figure 8.1 The conflict sequence

you may be driving the process but not be a direct party to it; while the phases are the same, your role may be different.

Recognize and flag the problem

Step one is recognizing the conflict and making it explicit. In distributed organizations conflict may be masked or even invisible to the leader. Individuals may be unwilling or unable to express the conflict, as they feel that it reflects badly on them.

Even when conflict is recognized, sometimes we learn to live with it and it becomes an unspoken part of the team dynamic.

In working with teams you sometimes stumble across unresolved conflicts. The team will be working on a particular issue quite happily and then suddenly, for no apparent reason, they will veer off and ignore an issue. Later, you will see the same thing again and you start to see a pattern. You may notice two individuals do not engage or that a particular topic seems to be off limits.

As an external person, one of the most positive things that you can do is to "put the cat on the table" by saying "it seems to me that there is some fundamental disagreement between A and B" or "every time we get to the issue of communication we seem to veer off and not want to deal with it, why is this?" Usually the team will look embarrassed and will start to talk about the underlying issue. Often they have resigned themselves to living with it and learned not to speak about it.

Team-building consultant, business services, Finland

For managers, it is useful to have a "trusted lieutenant" in the team or, even better, a culture in which individuals are encouraged to let managers know, confidentially, that there are unresolved conflicts.

Either way, until you recognize that you are in conflict and make it explicit, you are unlikely to be able to solve the issue.

Understand the differences

There are always at least two parties to a conflict; additionally, by the time it has become a conflict it has probably evolved from a discussion into an argument and people have developed fairly entrenched and emotional positions. Unless we understand and accept these different starting points, we will not be able to find common ground.

Different things are important to different people. Functional, cultural, and personal perspectives lead each of us to have a very different view of the world. People in finance, for example, have different training, a different self-image, pay attention to different business issues, and receive different information relevant to their roles than do people in sales or R&D, so of course their worldview will be different.

In a matrix, cross-functional and international cooperation implies that we are likely to deal more often with people who have widely contrasting views of the world. Opportunities for misunderstanding are far greater.

Step two is always to try and understand the thoughts, feelings, interests, and intentions of the other side. If you assume (their) positive intent, then you are more likely to find areas of agreement.

People in conflict often find themselves taking up opposite and mutually exclusive views of a problem. You need to move beyond this to find opportunities for mutual solutions.

Sometimes the conflict may be around a small issue. If a small problem is escalated, it may be a sign that some deeper need or issue lies behind it, unresolved. Do not stop at the surface symptoms; make sure that you have uncovered the real underlying problem.

It is important for each individual to accept what the other person is feeling. It is useful to acknowledge this by using accepting and neutral language, such as "I can see that you feel unhappy about this."

What is most important is to find out what the other person needs and why they need it.

Check for understanding by summarizing, wherever possible using their words, not yours.

If you are in conflict it is important first to walk a mile in the other person's shoes. If you still disagree, at least you are a mile away and you have got their shoes!

Tony Poots, trainer and consultant, UK

If you are one of the parties in conflict, it is also important to be honest about your feelings and perceptions; these are just as subjective as those of the other person. Are you clear about your real interests and needs?

Once these factors are out on the table, you need to step back, cool down, and achieve some perspective. It can be useful to reframe the perceptions to take out the emotions, look for objective information that tests the different perceptions, and try to identify common ground.

A useful technique can be to step outside the situation and tell the story of what happened as if you were relating it to a stranger. Creating a more neutral narrative script of the situation and its emotions can help bring a sense of perspective.

Individuals always act logically in their own terms. Sometimes this means them reinterpreting your actions to help them justify their own. If you can be clear and explicit about your motivations, it may help the other individuals to reframe their perceptions of you.

Create shared purpose

The purpose of understanding the differences in the previous phase is to identify common ground, common interests, wants, and needs. In the third stage you need to move the discussion forward by looking for areas of agreement on which to build.

You may find it useful to review some of the tools in Chapters 6 and 7 at this stage. Conflict tends to escalate and polarize views, so the tools on managing dilemmas and polarities and finding common interests will give you some frameworks for finding agreement and bridging differences.

Build and deliver agreement

The conflict sequence is not complete until you build specific agreements on how you will make sure that conflicts are resolved and do not reoccur. Agreement should be specific and actionable and you should monitor to see that agreements have been met in good faith.

As a manager, you would normally set both quantitative and qualitative targets and make sure that you review progress over time.

If individuals are unwilling to change their behavior or implement the agreements to which they have committed, it then becomes a performance-management or disciplinary problem rather than a conflict-management issue.

THE FIVE CONFLICT MODES

The Thomas-Kilmann Conflict Mode Instrument (TKI) is a model and questionnaire designed to measure how people behave in conflict situations. It is based around two axes: assertiveness and cooperativeness.

The model identifies five conflict styles:

❏ **Competing** – a person who pursues their own concerns at the other's expense.

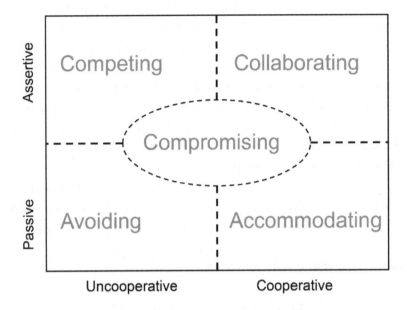

Figure 8.2 Thomas-Kilmann Conflict Modes Instrument

❏ **Accommodating** – an individual who sacrifices their own needs to satisfy those of the other.
❏ **Avoiding** – an individual who doesn't deal with conflict or withdraws.
❏ **Collaborating** – someone who works with the other to find a solution that satisfies both.
❏ **Compromising** – someone who tries to find some other way that partially satisfies each individual.

It is usually fairly straightforward to spot which style an individual is using:

❏ Competing and avoiding behaviors are unlikely to resolve serious conflicts or power struggles.
❏ Compromise can sometimes solve small issues, but each party has to be prepared to give up something, so the solution is often not optimal and may not be sustainable in ongoing relationships.
❏ Ideally, it is possible to find collaborative solutions that are stable and enduring.

You can use the Thomas-Kilmann questionnaire to identify an individual's natural styles in dealing with conflict and the model to discuss successful strategies toward which they can move when resolving conflict.

A key driver of people's engagement and effectiveness is the quality of their working relationships with their colleagues and boss. Conflict can be harder to identify and solve in a matrix, but we cannot allow it to go unrealized and unmanaged.

Use the information in this chapter to manage conflict more actively in your matrix team or organization. Do not allow conflicts to continue unresolved. If you cannot manage conflicts yourself using these tools, then bring in a mediator or other third party to help.

Before you leave this chapter

❏ Are there unresolved conflicts in your team or organization?
❏ Are they warranted or unwarranted?
❏ How can you manage storming and norming in your team?
❏ If you are in conflict, where are you in the conflict sequence and what needs to happen next?
❏ What styles do people use in managing conflict in your team? Do they work?

Part II
Cooperation

We set up a matrix to increase cooperation across the traditional silos of function and geography. However, if we are
not careful we see a sharp increase in the number of teams,
meetings, and calls when we move to a matrix organization.

Part II is about how we transform the cost and effectiveness of
cooperation in a matrix by being much more selective and clear
about the mode of working that will best achieve our objectives, and
by supporting cooperation through the use of social media and other
communication technologies.

In Part II:

9

More Cooperation
and Communication

Be careful what you wish for

One of the express objectives of most matrix structure implementations is to increase the amount of collaboration and communication across the traditional vertical silos. But be careful what you wish for!

In the early stage of implementation of a matrix, we nearly always see an increase in cooperation, in the form of more meetings, conference calls, and emails. The cost of cooperation also increases as teams become more complex and include participants from multiple sites, functions, cultures, and time zones.

In this chapter I will look at what is different about cooperation in a matrix, introduce four distinctly different "modes of working," and outline some principles for organizing cooperation more effectively in the matrix. The chapter covers:

❑ More complex cooperation – what is different in a matrix?
❑ The four buckets of cooperation
❑ Different goals need different ways of working
❑ Why size matters – the magic numbers of community

MORE COMPLEX COOPERATION – WHAT
IS DIFFERENT IN A MATRIX?

When I started my career, all of the members of my team worked in the same office. We were from the same culture and did similar jobs. We had a team meeting once a week. It was usually boring, but the cost was low and 30 minutes later we were back at our desks. If we needed an ad hoc meeting we could quickly gather people around.

Today, my team is spread around the world. With travel, accommodation, and time out of the office, a typical face-to-face meeting costs between $70,000 and $100,000. I have learned to be very selective about when this type of meeting really adds value.

Video, web, and phone conferences are less expensive, but are still difficult to arrange – coordinating diaries for busy people at short notice is next to impossible.

The obvious transaction costs such as travel and communication are very visible and tangible. Behind these are another set of costs that are less easy to quantify, but can have a real impact:

❏ Teams operate across barriers of distance and need to find ways of working together through technology.
❏ The requirement to work across complex organizational structures brings competition for both priorities and time.
❏ Time zones can introduce delay in decision making and communication.
❏ National, corporate, and functional cultural differences can introduce misunderstandings in communication styles and language.

For me, one of the biggest costs is the delay in decision making. Because the team feels responsible for key decisions, it has become impossible to make those decisions between meetings. We end up having to wait until everyone is in one place at one time to make critical decisions on our project.

Project manager, engineering, Sweden

If we do not learn to overcome these factors, we can experience delays to critical activities and decisions, additional costs, and increased dissatisfaction.

The good old days?

In the days before matrix working, most people belonged to "vertical" functions within geographies. A purchasing manager, for example, would be part of the purchasing function within a specific region or country – say, the USA – and report straight up to a purchasing director or VP.

There is a tendency for those now in a matrix structure to over-idealize the simplicity of the past and to blame the matrix structure for the complexity of today's business environment. The reality is that we were already busy, and we already faced complex challenges, tradeoffs, resource limitations, and internal conflicts. Then we introduced a matrix structure. In some cases, we formalized existing ad hoc or virtual relationships. In others, we added additional horizontal relationships and reporting lines.

I used to be busy enough before we introduced a matrix. Now I am also part of the business unit team, a supply chain team, and a virtual team sharing expertise with other purchasing professionals around the world, not to mention various ad hoc teams and projects. I continuously have to balance priorities.

In fairness, I used to work with most of these groups of people in the past, but they didn't have a "right to my time." All of them now see me as a formal part of their reporting and meeting relationships. All of these teams copy me on their emails and invite me to their team meetings, webinars, and conference calls. I have doubled the number of meetings and communications that I need to pay attention to.

Purchasing manager, retail, Spain

I used to report to the HR function, but now I am a business partner providing service to two business units. Both of these business units now invite me to their management meetings and conference calls and copy me on their emails. I also get invited by the functional groups within HR and my diary gets full very quickly. If I try and disconnect from these meetings, people seem to see it as a sign of disloyalty or lack of interest. The reality is I just do not have time for many of these meetings.

HR business partner, healthcare, USA

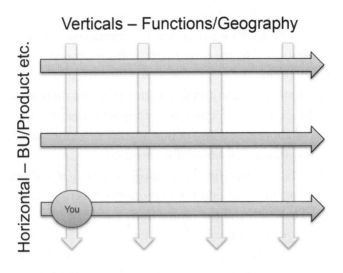

Figure 9.1 In the matrix

Typically, when the cost of something increases, economics tells us that the demand for it should fall. However, in a matrix implementation we often see both an increase in cost and complexity and an increase in the amount of cooperation and communication at the same time.

Companies often accompany a move to a more complex matrix way of working with a "one team" or "one company" campaign, designed to increase the amount of collaboration and coordination. This is rarely accompanied by an increased budget for travel, communication, or meetings, however.

How do we resolve this dilemma? We want more collaboration and communication, yet the volume and cost of this cooperation have increased markedly with global teams, multiple reporting lines, competing goals, and more diverse groups of colleagues in more locations.

In the early days of a matrix implementation, we should expect and encourage an increase in relationship building and communication as individuals build the new networks and connections that they require to get things done.

However, the risk is that this then becomes the norm and is embedded in our operating routines and governance. Once people are on distribution lists, meeting invites, and team rosters, it can be hard to get off them.

As we become more comfortable with a matrix structure, we then need to be much more selective in our use of teams, meetings, and other forms of cooperation and communication – otherwise we will be swamped with activity, often of poor quality.

Engaging people requires meaningful cooperation and real two-way communication, not endless low-quality meetings and broadcast emails. The quality of the interactions we create is critical to the degree of engagement we are able to attain.

We can transform the cost of cooperation and simplify our ways of working by being more selective about the specific form of cooperation we use.

THE FOUR BUCKETS OF COOPERATION

One of the most impactful ideas from my previous book, *Speed Lead*, was that not everything had to be done in teams. We realized that people use the word "team" when what they mean is cooperation. We also learned that there are much simpler ways to cooperate than by using traditional teams, which are tightly connected and require a great deal of synchronous communication, when everyone is available at the same time, if not the same place.

The idea of "star groups" (hub-and-spoke structures) and "spaghetti teams" (traditional, densely interconnected teams) really caught on with many of Global Integration's clients, and participants were able to use the concepts to significantly simplify the way they work together, as well as radically reducing the number of unnecessary meetings, conference calls, and emails. You will see detailed definitions of these modes of working later in this chapter.

It was a tremendous weight off my mind! I used to feel guilty that the people in my "team" did not see the value in our team meetings. It was like pulling teeth to get people to attend and I had constant complaints that the topics were rarely relevant to everyone attend-ing. When I understood that we were really a group rather than a team, I was able to change the way we communicated and save a lot of time. I make much better use of one-to-one communication now and satisfaction in my group has significantly increased.

Marketing manager, advertising, Singapore

In working with this idea with thousands of managers around the world, we found that most of them had never really challenged the idea of teams. They had never even entertained the idea that the costs of teaming could far outweigh the benefits.

I felt a bit nervous challenging the idea of teamwork. In my organization you are recruited for your ability to work in teams, it is one of the performance categories in our annual appraisal, and to be seen as "not a team player" is a kiss of death for your career. Without an alternative, my default had always been to encourage more teamwork. I have come to realize that teamwork wasn't always the right solution, I always felt guilty before when I couldn't make it work.

Field sales manager, FMCG, Italy

It was as if all cooperation was lumped together in one bucket and labelled "teamwork."

In our work we discovered that using simpler hub-and-spoke, star group ways of working proved to be more successful for the majority of tasks in distributed teams.

We also found that the existing quality of cooperation in organizations is low – partly because we try to manage all cooperation as if it were teamwork. Our course participants tell us that they spend on average two days a week in meetings and conference calls and that 50 percent of the content is irrelevant. That is a day per week of waste, every week, or nine years of unnecessary cooperation in a full career. One in five of our expensive management and professional people worldwide are tied up in unnecessary meetings and calls – permanently.

If I had a factory which was producing 50 percent scrap, I would close it down the following week – yet we routinely accept this level of quality in our meetings and communication.

Manufacturing director, automotive, USA

We have identified four distinctly different ways of working, four "buckets of cooperation" that make up the majority of cooperation in complex organizations:

❏ A **team** is a number of people with complementary skills working together closely to achieve a collaborative goal.
❏ A **group** is a number of individuals with either similar roles or skills, or complementary ones that do not require close collaboration but do need to be coordinated.
❏ A **community** is a group of people that share a sense of identity distinguishing them from the broader organization.
❏ A **network** is a number of people who are connected and related in some way. They are able to exchange information and may interact in order to achieve specific goals.

In the next chapter I will look in detail at each of these four ways of working and how we can manage each of them most effectively.

DIFFERENT GOALS NEED DIFFERENT WAYS OF WORKING

In the same way that structure should follow strategy at an organizational level, the way of working we choose should flow from the nature of the goal we are trying to achieve.

Teams, groups, communities, and networks are four distinct ways of cooperating, each of which is best suited to different sets of goals.

Make sure in your organization that the way of working you use is the one best suited to achieving your goal. In the absence of this clarity, companies tend to describe everything as a "team" and this can lead to unnecessary complexity in cooperation. Teams are best suited to small numbers of people and highly collaborative activities.

Mode of working	Typical goals	Example	Which of my activities should be managed in this way?
Team	Intensive collaboration to deliver a specific goal that requires multiple inputs; a team goal should be more than the sum of its individual parts	Multi-disciplinary problem-solving team	
Group	The coordination of individual efforts, often of individuals with similar skills and roles The output of the group is normally the sum of the output of the individuals within it	Coordination of a number of salespeople with similar skills and independent regions or clients	
Community	To focus on a particular domain or topic To create and sustain the identity of the community as a whole To develop the capability of its members and share learning and best practice To advance their common interests	A functional community such as the "purchasing community" in a large organization	
Network	To make it easy to connect with a range of individuals with whom you may want to engage in the future To maintain relationships through communication or connection To share information that may lead to deeper cooperation	LinkedIn or other social network	

WHY SIZE MATTERS – THE MAGIC NUMBERS OF COMMUNITY

In a matrix we may have to engage large numbers of people and so we need to understand how the number of people involved can also influence the way we organize.

In his book *How Many Friends Does One Person Need?* Robin Dunbar builds on his previous work on the size of effective communities. He previously identified "Dunbar's number," an effective limit to the number of coherent, face-to-face relationships that a human being can sustain of 150 people. He found that this was about the limit below which human societies could regulate themselves on the basis of relationships rather than the need for rules and hierarchy.

Bill Gore, founder of WL Gore, began his business in 1958 and developed the idea of a maximum site size of 150 people to support a nonhierarchical, relationship-based workplace. The company consistently ranks highly in "great place to work" surveys around the world.

In his new work, Dunbar identifies a series of other critical numbers in the structuring of human societies. These numbers can be found in anthropology, in the study of community sizes through history, in military organizations from the Romans to the present day, and right through to the structuring of modern organizations and social networks.

People tend to organize themselves in groupings of particular sizes:

❑ **3–6 people** – the typical number for a nuclear family, close friendship group, or a Special Forces team, and for effective spaghetti team working in our model.
❑ **10–15 people** – the typical size for an extended friendship group, a squad in the military, sports "teams," project groups, and a star group in our model.
❑ **50 people** – the size of a platoon in the military, the typical night camp in nomadic societies, and the size of an effective cloud community in our model.
❑ **150 people** – the size of a clan, a medieval village, or a company in the military, and an effective size for a purposeful network in our model.

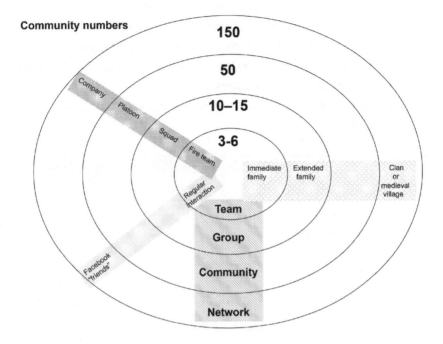

Figure 9.2   Community numbers

As we can see, the numbers tend to go up in factors of three. It is not clear why, but Dunbar believes that there are two key factors:

❑ The quality of relationships that we can sustain at each of these levels of intimacy – we can only hold a certain number of people at a particular intensity level.
❑ The time involved in maintaining contact at that level of relationship – we communicate more regularly and spend more time with people at the higher levels of intimacy.

These numbers are tremendously consistent in human societies. Try applying them to the structure of your organization.

Often we see a group of senior executives on the board (3 to 6 people) supported by 10 to 15 direct reports at the next level, heading up the operational regions, business units, and functions. We can then see a group around them of about 50 senior leaders, who take us down to the next level in the organization, and so on.

If these are the natural patterns of organization, it makes sense to incorporate this knowledge into the way we design our organizations and create effective work structures.

Where do these numbers occur naturally in your team or organization?

Mode of cooperation and size	Specific examples of these in my organization
Teams or subteams of 3–6	
Groups of 10–15	
Communities of up to 50	
Networks of up to 150	

Some of the additional challenges we have seen in matrix organizations may put these numbers under pressure:

❏ If one of the factors is the level of intimacy we can sustain in relationships, then the reduction in face-to-face time, less synchronous communication, and an increase in the diversity of colleagues may further limit the size of the teams, groups, and communities we can sustain.

❏ On the other hand, if the time and cost required to maintain relationships are limiting factors, then the rise of communications technology and social media may allow us to sustain larger networks and "shallow communities" by reducing the cost and complexity of staying in touch.

Interestingly, Dunbar identifies the typical number of friends on Facebook as 150, but if we look at how many people we actively engage with on a daily basis it is nearer to the 3–6 level. It is fascinating that we are even seeing these community patterns emerging in the world of social media.

Communications technology and social media do give us some opportunities to create the potential for connections and make relationship building easier and more cost effective. In Chapter 11 we will explore new ways of connecting our matrix teams, groups, communities, and networks to make cooperation more effective and reduce transaction costs.

Use the information in this chapter to increase your awareness of the danger of low-quality communication in the matrix and to start thinking about ways of cooperating other than teams.

In the next chapter we will look in detail at how we manage each of the four ways of working effectively.

Before you leave this chapter

❏ Have you seen an increase in cooperation and communication since you introduced a matrix?
❏ How much time do you spend on meetings, conference calls, and other collective communication?
❏ Of that time, how much of it is relevant to you?
❏ Are you using teams to address issues that are more suited to groups, communities, and networks?
❏ Where do you see the magic numbers of community in your organization?

10

The Four
Ways of Working

Spaghetti teams, star groups,
cloud communities, and
purposeful networks

Cooperation is vital to the success of a matrix organization. However, cooperation has become more complex and expensive. Too much of a focus on teamwork – a form of working in a matrix that is particularly expensive and hard to organize – can lead to poor-quality and unnecessary cooperation and communication, which can in turn undermine people's engagement and effectiveness.

In this chapter I will demonstrate when and how we should use each of the four ways of working – teams, groups, communities, and networks – for maximum success, and where we can combine them to get the best result. The chapter covers:

❏ Spaghetti teams
❏ Star groups
❏ Cloud communities
❏ Purposeful networks
❏ Mixed modes

These four ways of working are the building blocks of cooperation in any organization and need to be realigned and reengineered to support our matrixed way of working.

Using the right mode of cooperation for the right task can simplify cooperation and increase effectiveness as well as delivering the best results at the lowest cost.

The right mode can also be more engaging for people within the organization, because it allows us to cut out unnecessary meetings and speed up decision making – both common sources of frustration in large organizations.

I will introduce some guidelines on operating these modes of collaboration and try to deal with some myths and pitfalls regarding how they really work in complex organizations.

Remember, our objective is to streamline and realign our organization to make collaboration more effective and engaging, not to add 50 percent more ways to cooperate. At the same time as the matrix makes us more connected across the organization, we also need to be more selective about where we connect, or we will be swamped with poor-quality cooperation and communication.

It is just as important to find things we can *stop* doing as to discover new things we need to do.

I have given each of the ways of working a distinctive name and a specific definition. This is because I do not think these are clearly defined terms in our everyday work. My definitions are quite specific and are designed to help you select exactly the form of cooperation that will deliver your results most effectively.

Without this clarity, we can fall into the trap of applying the term "team" to everything from a small problem-solving group to an organization of thousands of people.

SPAGHETTI TEAMS

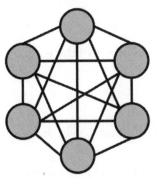

A spaghetti team is a number of people with complementary skills working together closely and interdependently to achieve a collaborative goal.

Purpose

The purpose of a team at work should be intensive collaboration to deliver a specific goal that requires multiple inputs.

A team goal should be more than the sum of its individual parts.

I am part of a really great team at the moment. It was put together to solve a particular business problem and it requires real multi-functional problem solving and detailed cooperation from all of us to solve the problem. We each bring different capabilities to the team as none of us can solve the problem on our own. We got to know each other well and built a really strong team spirit. It is probably my best experience of team working so far.

IT specialist, financial services, India

Ideal size

The ideal size for a team is 4–6 people. This gives sufficient diversity to open up discussions and provide different perspectives, but is not so large that participation and group dynamics become difficult.

Many organizational "teams" are larger than this – Global Integration's virtual teams survey shows that the average "team" size in the multinationals we work with is 11, and that individuals are typically members of five or more "teams."

Our recommendation, if you do have "teams" that are larger than 6 people, is that you look for opportunities to cluster them into smaller, more densely cooperative subteams.

Characteristics

Teams are characterized by:

❑ Objectives requiring cooperation of all members of the team.
❑ Individual roles that overlap.
❑ People who have complementary skills.
❑ Communication that is relatively frequent.
❑ People who are dependent on others in the team to get their daily work done.
❑ Information that is shared regularly because other members need it to do their work.

Workflow

Much of the work in a team is done synchronously – everyone is involved at the same time. True teamwork is characterized by highly participative meetings (face to face or through technology), where all people are present and engaged and working collaboratively on the same topic.

Team meetings should be focused on topics that are relevant to all members. The passive consumption of information such as PowerPoint presentations does not require teamwork, and handouts should be distributed in advance.

Teamwork implies interdependence and the existence of complementary skills. Individuals contribute different perspectives and capabilities to the team effort.

The team purpose cannot be met by an individual or a subset of the team or by handing the work sequentially from one to the other; everyone needs to be engaged and contributing to success. When done well, teamwork produces synergy above and beyond the individual contributions of the team members.

High-performing teams bring a range of perspectives to business problems, they are enjoyable and memorable to work in, and they produce a strong shared spirit.

Disadvantages

Because of the close working relationships in teams, individuals need to get to know each other and develop shared ways of working. This means adapting your work style and pace to others in the team. As a result, teams have to dedicate time and resources, particularly at the early stage, into internal dynamics. This is energy and time they are not using to move toward their goal.

The historical definition of the word team is "two or more animals harnessed together to draw a vehicle or plough." Teams bring constraint as well as opportunity and we should only use them when the opportunity is greater than the costs and constraints involved.

In global and virtual organizations, the transaction costs of teamwork have increased steeply. As a result, our use of teamwork needs to be more discerning.

STAR GROUP

A star group is made up of a number of individuals with either similar roles or skills, or complementary ones that do not require close collaboration but do need to be coordinated.

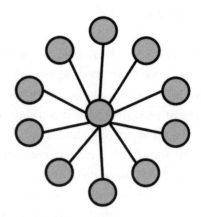

Purpose

The purpose of a group at work should be the coordination of individual effort. The output of the group is normally the sum of the output of the individuals within it.

> *I manage what I used to call a sales team, but which I now know is a group. Individuals have similar skills and their own territories. We used to have team meetings where we shared activity updates. We learned that these were largely irrelevant to the other individuals. I now focus on one-to-one communication with individuals and, on the rare occasions when we do get together, we only focus on areas where we really have a shared need – such as common training or celebrating success.*
>
> Sales manager, technology, USA

Ideal size

The ideal size for a group is 10–15 people.

Groups can grow larger than teams, depending on the capabilities of the individuals and the leader. They are not limited by the need to run effective synchronous meetings and calls, or by the team dynamics that make collective working more complex.

Characteristics

Groups are characterized by:

❏ People who are normally working on individual objectives.
❏ Roles that do not overlap.
❏ People who have unique skills.
❏ Communication that is relatively infrequent.
❏ People who can normally complete their daily work without information or service from others in the group.
❏ Work that may be passed on from one member of the group to another.
❏ Information that is shared for learning and interest.

Workflow

The typical workflow in a group is one to one. Individuals have autonomous jobs and are coordinated by a common leader. Work may be passed on from one group member to another in sequence, but the group members are rarely all working collaboratively at the same time on the same piece of work.

Groups thrive on one-to-one contact and this does not always have to be via a central point. Groups need the discipline and relationships that allow communication to flow between individuals when the, relatively infrequent, need for communication arises.

Because of this, communication in a group is easy to schedule. For one-to-one communication we just pick up the phone to the individual we want to talk to. We do not need to coordinate multiple diaries and we can pick the most convenient time to talk across time zones and other commitments.

Asynchronous working is more common, so we can use email, social media, and other tools to communicate, since they do not rely on us being in the same "place" simultaneously.

There are relatively few reasons to get all the members of a group together at the same time, in fact. In general, communication will flow through the center or through one-to-one conversations with group members.

Leaders of groups often use meetings to make sure that communication is received equally by all members. In theory, this information could be provided by email or other asynchronous means. However, if it is vital that the information gets to everyone at the same time, a synchronous conference call may be necessary.

Because group members have similar skills, they will probably have common training needs. Group meetings may be used for skills training or to ensure the common implementation of new processes and tools.

Individuals in a group need to know each other well enough and trust each other so that the communication flow is easy. They need to be able to pick up the phone without any barriers to communicating one to one. Group meetings should include an element of relationship building and maintenance – particularly if there are new group members.

Disadvantages

Groups may suffer from duplication of effort if the person in the center does not identify issues of common interest or spread common learning.

Individuals may feel disconnected from their colleagues unless there are sufficient relationship-building opportunities in the group.

A particular problem with group meetings is that the group leader often feels that it should be run as a team. As a result, regular "team meetings" are held. For the individual at the center everything may be relevant, but it is highly likely in a group that discussions will only be relevant to one individual and the manager, so the other members waste a great deal of time listening to irrelevant information sharing – particularly status updates.

CLOUD COMMUNITY

A cloud community is a group of people who share a sense of identity that distinguishes them from the broader organization.

The name implies a shared culture, history, or interest. In the past it implied a sense of location, although not necessarily today.

Purpose

The purposes of a community at work are:

❑ To focus on a particular domain or topic.
❑ To create and sustain the identity of the community.
❑ To develop the capability of its members – to share learning and best practice.
❑ To advance their common interests.

We hold an annual get-together of the HR community. It is really nice to meet up with people who share some common interests and a sense of identity as HR professionals. It is important to create connections and get to know people, but there are relatively few topics where all of us are equally engaged and interested.

We focus on some common training issues, but when we get down into the detail of our work – organization development, talent management or compensation and benefits, for example – people have different interests.

At that point we typically break into smaller groups to focus on the specific areas of interest – otherwise we would be listening to presentations and discussions on topics that were not relevant to all of us.

HR director, business services, Hungary

Ideal size

An ideal size for a community is up to 50 people.

Communities based on a location (communities of place) can be larger, as the transaction costs of connection are lower and community building tends to happen as a free by-product of being in the same location.

Communities that are connected online or through social media enjoy similar reductions in costs of connection, although the degree of connection and shared identity may be less "deep."

Characteristics
....

Communities are characterized by:

❑ A sense of common identity and distinctness from the surrounding organization that has meaning to the members.
❑ Shared values and a sense of social cohesion.
❑ Boundaries, so that it is clear who is not a member.
❑ Possibly voluntary in nature – gathered around a shared social interest, location, or common interest – or defined by the organization – "the finance community" or more formal "communities of practice" in areas such as project management.
❑ At a minimum, common interests.

We are all members of several possible communities, for example defined by culture, religion, sports, hobbies, function, location, and company. However, we do not feel the same sense of identification with all of these communities. For each of us, one is more important than the others and we identify with this particular community more strongly.

Strong communities often have distinct boundaries. Occupational or functional communities create a language, a jargon, and a set of symbols such as uniforms. Production shift workers, for example, often form strong communities because they have leisure time when other people are at work, so they tend to socialize more with other shift members.

A traditional community of practice might be a guild or a craft, for which there are initiation ceremonies, myths, heroes, and long training periods. This is partly about creating barriers to entry and exclusivity. Traditionally such communities were used to keep pay rates high, as they still do in professions such as medicine and the law.

These boundaries and distinct identities can, however, become a problem when we start to work across organizational boundaries. In my cross-cultural practice I have often found overcoming functional cultures to be more of a challenge than dealing with national cultural differences within teams. For example, it can be easier to get salespeople from around Europe to cooperate than salespeople and finance people within the same country.

Communities of practice

Communities of practice are a specific type of community organized around interest and identity. They exist to do a number of things:

❑ To focus on a particular area or domain of knowledge or expertise.
❑ To identify common practices; the best ways to get things done; the shared sets of approaches, issues, tools, and problems that people need to understand or use to be effective.
❑ To identify expertise and make it visible to the community – who to go to when you have a problem.
❑ To create a sense of social identity, and shared values and behaviors.

Communities have traditionally had a "place" that provided a mechanism for people to meet. Increasingly, that place is not only face to face but also online. We need to provide facilities for these communities to form and thrive.

Communities often emerge from within larger networks of people who have common interests, or who find some value in cooperation. These people may spontaneously organize meetings or events and attract others who see the value of interacting with them. They are frequently the thought leaders, or those with energy or passion around an issue.

Successful communities require a pattern of connection, some kind of rhythm of communication that allows them to interact regularly enough to sustain the community. This might be a pattern of regular events, some face to face, interspersed with local community events, global community events, a technology space, and increasingly a social media presence.

Communities require some form of facilitation: someone to seed ideas, create connections, carry out work between meetings, and make sure that there is a framework sustaining the communication and the community. This is particularly important if value may not immediately be clear when the community meets for the first time. There needs to be value in cooperation as seen from the point of view of the community members, otherwise why would they engage?

Communities are about creating opportunities for connection and dialogue and seeing what emerges. They are not about forcing collaboration.

In 2011 Global Integration sponsored Tweet Camp, one of Europe's leading Twitter conferences. The organizers created random table groups and posted questions like "How are you using Twitter?" and "What do you see as the opportunities for the future?" Each table generated ideas for further discussion and people could sign up to sessions they wanted to attend.

In each discussion we typically found someone who had a shared interest and we would quickly exchange hashtags and Twitter names. Some of the groups contained a core of individuals who kept in touch afterward and were motivated to continue to explore opportunities. It was a good example of allowing cooperation to emerge without forcing it.

Expect different levels of participation in communities, particularly if they are online. Jakob Nielson, a usability guru, says that in any online community, 90 percent of people are "lurkers" who just visit and read others' contributions, 9 percent sometimes contribute, and 1 percent account for most contributions in the community.

Also be aware that it is not only the public events that make the community work. Public events are there to create connections and encourage one-to-one interactions or small groups to take issues away and work on them privately. Facilitation that enables and encourages this is important.

Communities develop and evolve as the membership and the environment change, therefore they need to be dynamic and focused on recruiting new members as the environment adapts.

For more on communities of practice, read *Cultivating Communities of Practice* by Etienne Wenger, Richard McDermott, and William Snyder.

Workflow

Workflow in a community is focused on maintaining relationships and the shared feeling of common interest in the group: the transmission of identity and values.

At the point at which there is a need to do something – act on common interests, share learning, or do something in the interest of the community – a team or group will often form to get things done.

Functional communities within an organization tend to focus on capability building, common practices, shared problems, and professional development, such as making sure that there are sufficient trained accountants for the future needs of the organization.

In our organization most of the work is delivered by individuals and groups. We invest in community-building activities to make sure that the relationships are in place, so that if people need to pick up the phone to call a colleague there are no barriers to doing so and individuals will be likely to cooperate.

It is unlikely that all members of the community will work together cooperatively on a particular topic. Usually when actual work needs doing a team of volunteers will come forward.

Community leader, business services, China

Be careful of trying to impose communities rather than letting them emerge.

One objective of our global matrix was to share resources and identify synergies across our purchasing organization. There were some very obvious opportunities to share purchasing on one of our key components. We quickly put a team together in one specific area and identified over $20 million of savings by coordinating our buying.

We then got very excited and brought our purchasing community together at a worldwide meeting. We set up formal teams in a wide range of areas and asked them to work on common purchasing projects. Unfortunately, we did not identify many opportunities; a lot of what we buy is best bought locally. We spent a lot of time and money bringing together global teams for not a lot of benefit in these areas.

Global head of purchasing, brewing, USA

One of the US members of my team asked if we could have a global training community meeting. We met at year end and had a fabulous meeting in Vienna; there was lots of mutual respect, common interests and fun – everything, in fact, apart from an output!

When they asked for another meeting the following year, I refused. Instead, I gave funding to a number of smaller global teams who had to collaborate on a common goal – to produce a common global leadership program or a common ethics program. These were much more productive.

Training director, electronics, Netherlands

Instead of forcing cooperation, Global Integration works with communities to "seed the cloud." At a large meeting of the technical stewardship function in an FMCG organization, we ran a conference that incorporated trade shows, small round tables with company experts, and whiteboard rooms where people could capture their ideas.

We seeded a number of topics and themes and got the participants to move around, spending as much or as little time as they liked on each topic. The ones who were engaged and motivated and saw real business opportunities signed up to continue to be involved in these topics. Many did not, but the ones who did were willing volunteers who perceived real value in collaboration. This approach tends to be more effective than top-down, mandated improvement teams.

Face-to-face community meetings should typically focus on reinforcing identity and creating relationships within the community so that, in normal day-to-day operations, people know and trust each other well enough that there are no barriers to deeper communication and cooperation when they become necessary.

Disadvantages

If communities are not well structured, they can lose relevance and focus. If the membership is too diverse, then they will share too little to enable stimulating conversations and connections.

Communities that become talking shops without any tangible actions or progress quickly wither away; we are all too busy for another talking shop.

If they lose focus, communities can be hijacked by people with particular passions and interests and focus on topics that are only of interest to those individuals or a small subset of the community. It is important to concentrate on the activities or issues that are truly of common interest.

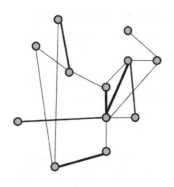

PURPOSEFUL NETWORKS

A purposeful network is a number of people who are connected and related in some way. They are able to exchange information and may interact in order to achieve specific goals. A network is made up of the people and the pattern of connections and interactions between them.

Purpose

The purposes of a network are:

❏ To connect and stay connected with a range of people you may want to engage with more deeply in future.
❏ To maintain these relationships with some form of connection or communication.

Each of us has several professional networks – to advance our career, for learning, or to get things done in our current role. These will have varying goals and will be managed differently.

Ideal size

The ideal size for a network is up to 150 people.

Characteristics

Networks are characterized by:

❏ The members.
❏ The patterns of relationships and other connections between them.
❏ The interactions between the people and their patterns of connections.

People often think of networking as having a coffee and handing out business cards. In complex organizations, networks, not the formal structure, shape how things really get done.

Networks need to be formally established around specific goals, and they have to be maintained and engaged as an everyday part of getting work done – that is why we call this way of working *purposeful* networking.

A network provides the potential for collaboration. At the point at which the network is activated to get something done, it will probably migrate to either one-to-one contact or a team or group mode of cooperation.

Connections between secondary members of the network may be weak or nonexistent, as distinct from a community, in which people tend to share more common interests.

A network is focused on the individual's pattern of one-to-one relationships. The individual is at the center of a network.

Workflow

The typical workflow in a network is an individual reaching out to one or more network members with a request for information or assistance. Responses normally come to the individual initiating the request, or may be shared with other network members too.

Online networks allow us to have a personal profile page and the ability to connect simply with other individuals, and they offer a low-cost way of sharing and commenting on information that is circulated by other network members.

Senior people often have high levels of connectivity; they tend to have longer experience and more opportunities to meet face to face with peers and others from across the organization.

To be honest, the move to a matrix has not made a great differ-ence. I have been in the business a long time and have worked in a number of different functions and business units. The senior group has regular retreats and planning sessions, so we really get to talk through and nail down some of the issues. It is also good to get time to socialize in the evenings of these events and to keep building our networks. Working in a matrix is not so different.

Business unit head, power engineering, Malaysia

We have seen how important the "matrixed middle" is to a successful matrix. We should ensure there are also opportunities for this group to build and maintain the networks they need to succeed.

I am based in Brazil. A lot of my activities are local, but I am also matrixed in to both the regional and global marketing organiza-tions. It is rare that I meet my colleagues outside of the region. When we do get together, it tends to be in very large groups and there is not much time for networking.

It is only during the breaks and evenings in occasional meet-ings that I get to connect face to face and meet new people in my function.

You can get things done through technology, of course, but you do need relationships to resolve conflicts and a good network for when new issues come up and you need help.

This makes the global matrix more challenging for me.

Marketing manager, pharmaceuticals, Brazil

If there aren't enough network connections and opportunities at middle levels, the organization can experience high levels of escalation to more networked senior people in order to get things done.

People tend naturally to build networks based on proximity. In a matrix there are many opportunities to broaden your network across traditional vertical silos, but you do need to capitalize on these opportunities.

Given that networking is relatively difficult and expensive in distributed organizations, time and space must be allowed to enable it.

MIXED MODES

I have described four pure modes of working: teams, groups, communities, and networks. In the real world we operate at different times in different modes. We do, however, need to remain clear on what mode we are using for a particular task, so that we can employ the most effective way of working for each.

A common example is a global project team, which may act as a spaghetti team in the early stages to ensure that the kickoff is clear and goals and objectives are aligned. However, once they start to deliver the work, most activity is performed in group mode. Individuals have their own unique goals and coordinate relatively infrequently or on a one-to-one basis as required. They may come together in team mode infrequently to solve particular multidisciplinary problems, or to replan important milestones, celebrate success, or share learning.

The risk is that, having started as a team, the global project members then assume that everything has to be done as a team. In this case, progress between meetings and calls tends to be slow. "We cannot make a decision until the next meeting" is a common refrain.

In my experience, the majority of distributed virtual teams spend most of their time working as a group and have relatively infrequent needs to act as a team.

Use the information in this chapter to ensure that you are clear about the form of cooperation you need and to organize in the simplest way that will enable you to get things done.

By systematically identifying where you need to build new teams, groups, communities, and networks, you can increase cooperation across historical vertical silos without adding unnecessary cost and complexity.

In the next chapter I will look at how we can use communication technology and social media to support each mode of working.

Before you leave this chapter

❑ Are you using teams to get things done that could be done more simply by groups or other forms of cooperation?
❑ Do you have the teams, groups, communities, and networks in place that you need to be successful in your matrix?
❑ Are you using the right form of cooperation, given your goals and the number of people involved?
❑ Do the members of your teams, groups, communities, and networks have a clear understanding of how to organize their particular ways of working effectively?

11

Cooperating through Technology and Social Media

Connecting with colleagues, followers, and friends

Communications technology allows matrix organizations and virtual teams to exist and to succeed. It is a critical enabler of cooperation and reduces the transaction costs of working with colleagues in other locations.

At the same time, communication through technology is a barrier that we need to overcome to achieve effective cooperation. We receive a large volume of irrelevant communication and our engagement is reduced when we have to sit through boring webinars and unnecessary late-night conference calls.

In this chapter I will identify which specific technologies are best for supporting each of the four ways of working (teams, groups, communities, and networks) and how we can improve the relevance of communication and engagement in online communication. I will also look at the emerging promise of social media and how it can support matrix working. The chapter covers:

❏ Using communications technologies to support the four ways of working
❏ Improving the relevance of communication
❏ Creating participation and engagement online
❏ The promise of social media

USING COMMUNICATIONS TECHNOLOGIES TO SUPPORT THE FOUR WAYS OF WORKING

Ensuring that individuals have access to communications technologies and the skills necessary to use them properly is essential for effective cooperation in distributed teams and organizations. But which technologies are most effective in supporting each of the four modes of working?

Spaghetti team technologies

Synchronous working requires spaghetti team members to be available at the same time, if not in the same place, in order to achieve a truly collaborative goal. Real teamwork takes place in face-to-face meetings and through tools like video conferencing, audio conferencing, and webinars, which allow for simultaneous participation.

Teams require shared access to common documents and the ability to work on them collaboratively, so wikis and shared spaces are essential.

Nevertheless, the big communication challenge in teams lies in creating synchronous participation and engagement, particularly when communicating through technology (more on this later in the chapter).

Our team was working on a complex multidisciplinary task where people had a lot of passion and strong views about the solutions. Everyone wanted to have their say and some of the best ideas came out of these interactions.

While we found this relatively easy to manage face to face, it was really hard by audio conference and webinar. Interruptions were common and the discipline of a call tended to fall. The ability to air views and be listened to became a real problem for our global team. We found we could only make it work with very small groups, maybe even of two to three people.

Project leader, advertising, USA

I am part of a regular "team" conference call with 20 participants. There is relatively little opportunity for discussion; it tends to be one individual giving information to the rest of us, with limited opportunity to ask questions. I now realize we are operating in group mode, not as a team.

In fact, a lot of the information shared on these calls could be sent to us for reading. This would be better than me joining the call at 10 pm from home.

Software manager, telecoms, Hong Kong

Working through technology imposes additional constraints on team size. As teams grow, they quickly find it difficult to have true collaborative discussions through audio conferencing and similar tools. Larger teams effectively operate as groups when working together through technology.

Micro blogging tools such as Twitter or others like Instant Messenger can be useful for sharing short updates or questions with team colleagues in real time.

Because teams tend to have a longer lifetime, they usually develop a social component. Social media can be used to reinforce this, with individuals sharing information of common interest about work issues, but also about external interests and perspectives.

Having access to this information in the team-formation stage can accelerate relationship building by identifying areas of common interest. Something as simple as sharing photos helps relationships form more quickly.

On the first day I joined the team, I was able to check out my new colleagues' internal Facebook profiles. I could get a sense for their style of operating, who were the regular contributors, the relationships within the team, and also find out a little bit about them as individuals.

It was really helpful because I did not get to meet some of them for nearly six months. Despite this, I felt that even emails were better because I had a sense of the individual. I could also get a feeling for the "story" of the activities of the team by looking at the history of the activities on the blog and also access up-to-date documents. My previous company didn't have these tools and I found them to be really helpful.

Regulatory affairs manager, healthcare, Belgium

Star group technologies

The main mode of communication in a group is one to one, to ensure coordination of goals and activities. Telephone, desktop video, web meetings, and Instant Messenger are useful for synchronous one-to-one communication.

Groups may require shared access to common documents, so wikis and shared spaces are useful.

The big communication challenge in groups is spotting what relevant information needs to be shared and making sure that it is shared effectively, without making everyone sit through collective updates of limited interest.

While groups do not need a high level of social contact to be effective, it is important to maintain the quality of relationships and a sense of belonging, so that individuals know and trust each other enough to be able to pick up the phone and get help when they need it.

Social media is useful in maintaining this relatively infrequent but important social contact. It also enables us to have a richer understanding of our colleagues when we may not have a great deal of face-to-face time together.

I get a lot of emails from my colleagues telling me what they are working on and few of them are relevant. I rely on the one-to-one calls with my boss to draw my attention to things that are important.

Mostly when I discuss issues with her they are only relevant to the two of us. Occasionally she will point to other people in the group who have similar issues or solutions to my problems and that is really useful.

It is also clear in our group who has the most experience and expertise in specific areas. I know if I need support in event management, for example, I can call VJ in India directly and he will help me out.

Marketing associate, FMCG, Russia

Effective group working is also supported by a move away from push technologies like email, where information is sent out for everyone to read, toward pull technologies such as shared spaces, where information is available for those who need it. Broadcast emails can be of low relevance to group members and may regularly be ignored. When an individual has an issue or problem, it is essential that they know where to look.

Cloud community technologies

Communication in a cloud community is based either on sustaining the community itself or on advancing the particular knowledge, capabilities, or interests of the community members.

Social media is ideal for supporting community building and maintenance. It is a low-cost way of sharing information of common interest and people can choose only to subscribe to information that they personally find relevant. It also enables other community members to identify experts on specific topics and to engage with them easily.

Membership of online communities can be restricted if necessary and shared spaces can be used to store relevant information and updates that may not be of immediate need, but could be of future use to community members.

These community spaces are an effective alternative to push emails for updates on subjects such as training, new developments, and research papers. Such information may be important, but does not require people to be interrupted from their current work.

A community discussion area, focused on a particular practice or capability, can be a good place to store key documents and learning aids and allows for community discussions about what members are finding works well, new developments, or links to interesting articles or videos.

We do not meet very often, but we all share some common tools and approaches that we use in our training programs. We used to share these in face-to-face discussions and get into long conversations about "I do this, why do you do that." People could get a bit defensive if others didn't pick up their ideas. Now we have a social media tool where we have the chance to upload our own photos, images, flipchart pictures, or anything we think is helpful in explaining the tools and concepts. We can add audio clips of our latest ideas or relevant articles or YouTube videos we think can illustrate the learning points effectively.

This is really useful for new people, but also helps when we want to update our core materials. We can quickly see any new ideas or ways of using the materials.

VP global learning and development, entertainment, UK

It is very easy for us to identify the "hot button" issues in our community. You can see who other people are choosing to follow and what topics are trending as important. If there is a critical mass of interest in an issue, we can also see who the opinion leaders are and who has the energy around the topic. We may ask them to lead a specific piece of work that needs doing. It allows issues and leaders to emerge rather than us having to force them from the top down.

Product development director, software, USA

It is also common in organizational communities such as those based on functions to offer common events around issues of widespread interest to their members, or for transmitting time-sensitive information such as business updates or organizational changes.

We have a quarterly HR community call. There are about 40 of us on the call, so there is limited opportunity for interactivity. They tend to start with a business update, which is a chance for us all to get up to date with the current thinking of our HR head and business priorities. We also have a guest speaker who will talk on a specific issue of general relevance – for example an organizational change or a new training initiative for the HR group itself. They only last an hour and we can ask questions if we want to.

HR director, financial services, India

Purposeful network technologies

Communication in a purposeful network usually involves setting up and maintaining individual network relationships and then sharing information with the members of your network.

Tools such as LinkedIn support business networking by making it easy and inexpensive to connect to other people. Information can be broadcast to network members and it is relatively straightforward to search for specific individuals or characteristics through their profiles.

> *I have a large network on LinkedIn, well over 500 people. It is a great way of staying in contact with a highly mobile group of clients and past contacts. They may forget to let me know their new contact details, but they usually remember to update LinkedIn. Some of the tools like Trip Advisor are good for letting me know when I am in the same location as some of my contacts and have sparked face-to-face conversations or meetings.*
>
> *I do not really pay attention to the status updates, as there are just too many of them. I keep in active contact with a much smaller group, usually sending them something by email or calling them from time to time to catch up.*
>
> VP, global consulting, UK

Once a concrete need for cooperation emerges from the network, it will normally evolve into a one-to-one conversation, team, or group to get things done.

In *Speed Lead* I wrote about choosing and using the right communications technology for the task. Since then, most of Global Integration's clients have invested in a full range of communications technologies. Virtual team members have become much more comfortable with communication through technologies such as email, web conferencing, and video.

The table is a summary of the best forms of communications technology for each mode of organizing.

Mode of cooperation	Synchronous, face to face	Synchronous through technology	Asynchronous through technology
Team	Team meetings	Web meetings Video conferencing Conference calls Instant Messenger	Email Shared files Social media spaces
Group	One-to-ones Group meetings on common issues only	One-to-one calls Desktop video Instant Messenger	Email Shared files Social media spaces Broadcasts
Community	Community events and meetings	Online "conferences" Micro blogging Webinars	Social media spaces Shared files Community discussion areas
Network	Networking events	Online "conferences" Micro blogging	Connection tools Profiles Social media spaces

Two of the biggest challenges that we see individuals struggling with in using communications technology today are how to improve relevance and participation.

IMPROVING THE RELEVANCE OF COMMUNICATION

Participants in our virtual teams survey tell us that they receive around 60 emails a day and that only about 25 percent of these are really necessary for them to do their jobs. They spend two days a week in meetings and conference calls, of which 50 percent are irrelevant.

This is an enormous source of waste and frustration and could be costing large organizations over 20 percent of their management and professional wage bill. For a company with 10,000 employees, 30 percent of whom experience this level of unnecessary meetings and emails, this would cost $60 million a year, every year.

Given the scope of this waste and the impact on people engagement and productivity, it always surprises me that companies do not allocate more attention to managing this issue. If we were wasting $60 million a year in most other areas of business we would be working hard to drive it out. In cooperation and communication, most companies simply accept a day per week of waste as normal.

Because irrelevant cooperation is such a time stealer, it is worth the initial investment of some time with your team or department to identify how relevant meetings, conference calls, emails, and other forms of communication are to the recipients. Eliminating unnecessary communication could save you a day a week.

Here are my top four tips to improve the relevance of communication in your team, group, network, or community.

Choose the right way of working

If we think that cooperation is all about teamwork, then we will tend to share large amounts of information. In a team, we need to know what our colleagues are thinking about and working on because we are deeply interdependent.

However, in groups, communities, and networks we need to share far less information. By choosing simpler ways of working we will learn that we do not need to share so much.

Move from push to pull

Push forms of communication such as email are sent to recipients because the sender thinks that the information they contain is important. They tend to interrupt and distract the recipient. Pull communication posts information in shared spaces and community areas so that it is available for those who need it and choose to seek it out.

Because individuals then decide for themselves what is important, they pull only information that is relevant to them.

Dare to disconnect

Take the time to disconnect from distribution lists and sources of information that you do not really need. This is a continual process, as people consistently feel that you should know things that you do not need to know.

Schedule time to block senders, get off distribution lists, and give feedback to people who send you information you do not need. The alternative is to be swamped with irrelevant information that gets in the way of you seeing the things to which you really need to pay attention.

Use social filtering

You can use social media such as Twitter to get feedback on what is worth paying attention to. If you follow someone you trust, or who has expertise in a particular area, then they will flag up topics, articles, or issues that are worth you giving some attention to in their area of expertise. For example, if you follow @GlobalInteg on Twitter or join our "Matrix Management" LinkedIn group, we will flag up interesting articles or resources on matrix management.

If other people like you are paying attention to something, then it is more likely to be relevant to you, too.

CREATING PARTICIPATION AND ENGAGEMENT ONLINE

If your face-to-face meetings and presentations are boring and lack participation, then buying tools such as WebEx or NetMeeting will just mean that you can bore a larger population of people at a slightly lower cost!

In all my years of training, I never met anyone who said "I wish we had more meetings and presentations to look at," but many people who ask for more one-on-one time, more real conversations with their boss and close colleagues. Building real engagement means creating two-way communication where people can be listened to and ask questions.

Global Integration puts a lot of focus into creating participation and engagement in our face-to-face training programs and we have successfully applied these same principles to creating participation in web conferences.

Here are our key principles for encouraging participation online and offline:

❑ Focus on the audience. Usually there is only one presenter or chairperson but many more participants. Is the session a good use of their time, do they all need to be there?

❑ For each topic, learning point, or agenda item, ask "How can we make it participative?" Check what participants are doing at each stage of the process. If the answer is "shutting up and listening to me," then reconsider.

❑ Get people participating quickly. If you present for two hours where participants have no role but to sit and listen, do not be surprised if you get few questions and little interaction at the end – you have trained them to remain silent and passive.

❑ Get people involved in the generation and creation of materials and ideas rather than just presenting finished ideas and materials to them. Get people to write on flipcharts, screens, or other materials and come up with their own ideas and solutions.

❑ Engage all the senses. Use color and music. Encourage movement by getting people to walk around and post things on the walls. In conference calls and webinars, have regular breaks for movement.

❑ Make the room layout match the process of the meeting. If you walk into a darkened room with rows of chairs pointed at a brightly lit stage, the message is clear: participants are here to listen and not to distract the presenter at the front. Small round tables encourage participation and group discussion. If the "room" is virtual, keep numbers small and provide for subgroups and breakout sessions.

If you find that there is little role for participation in your meeting, then why not cancel it and send an email with an attachment of your content instead?

It is possible to take the principles and philosophies behind these ideas and apply many of them to synchronous online communication.

In creating participation online, first we need to understand the technology and the opportunities it gives us. Most web conferencing tools, for example, provide significant opportunities to create engagement and participation – but only if we plan for it in advance. It is very difficult to create spontaneous participation with these tools.

First, check that your people have been trained in the technology. It is quite common in our workshops to find that fewer than 20 percent of the people in an organization that actively uses tools like WebEx or NetMeeting have ever been formally trained to use the system. Most providers give access to free or inexpensive online training and in many cases you can learn all you need to know in about 45 minutes. If people are not aware of the technical opportunities and limitations of the tool, there will always be a barrier to communication. Get the knowledge barrier out of the way early by insisting that people are trained.

Once you have overcome the technology barrier, the key challenge lies in creating engagement and participation. With a little planning you can incorporate some or all of the following tips into the way you run your online events. Here are my top 10 participation and engagement tools for online meetings:

1. **Polling** – pose a question and give real-time feedback on the results. Example: "How many emails do you receive per day and how many are relevant?"

2. **Voting** – either through a poll or the "raise your hand" or yes/no function in most webinar tools. Example: "Have you received the organization's announcement on the new matrix structure?"

3. **Subgroups** – in some systems you are able to allocate subgroups and give them a separate conference call number, so that they can have side discussions and report back to the main group. Example: "Team A, please consider your answer to question 1 and create a slide of your ideas to share with us when we resume

as a full group in 10 minutes; team B, take question 2." Smaller subgroups improve participation levels.

4. **Screen sharing** – you can break a presentation slide into several segments and ask individuals to type their responses on the screen. Example: "Type what you see as the advantages of the matrix organization in the top-left quadrant and the disadvantages in the bottom-right quadrant."

5. **Handing over control** – allow individuals to take control of particular segments and add their comments or inputs to shared documents or applications.

6. **Take regular breaks** – I recommend no more than an hour of continuous webinar or conference call. Ideally, limit the entire session to one hour. Participation levels fall fast if online events or calls go on too long. For cross-cultural, multilingual groups, make breaks even more frequent to give people time to process the material and to rest. Participating in a second or third language is tiring.

7. **Enable questions** – have a mechanism for asking questions, either by the "raise your hand" function or through chat. It is quite hard to monitor chat or questions while running a webinar, so it is useful to have a colleague who checks these for you and feeds you any specific questions that need to be answered during the breaks. Pause regularly and ask for questions.

8. **Use materials that call for interaction** – get participants to fill in slides and type answers to questions so that they have some kind of physical activity to perform, rather than falling back into the passive viewing of content that someone else has created.

9. **Limit audience size** – the larger the audience, the easier it is for participants to hide and the harder it is to involve everyone. You should limit participation to the minimum number of people required to meet your objective. If you require real teamwork, limit the audience to 3–6 participants.

10. **Keep a list of participants** – each time an individual contributes, put a tick against their name. If an individual is not participating, you could ask them a question or send them a message.

Remember to plan participation and engagement in advance by concentrating on the participant experience. If you only use tools like WebEx as online page-turners to give presentations, you will find that people are not really paying attention. In face-to-face meetings we may have to pretend to look interested for reasons of politics or politeness. If an online presentation is boring, we will read our emails or check Facebook instead.

THE PROMISE OF SOCIAL MEDIA

As I write this, the use of social media inside organizations is relatively new. There is tremendous hype about the development of "social business," yet many employers still block access to sites like Facebook and YouTube over concerns that employees will waste time or damage their company's reputation with unguarded comments.

Nevertheless, I believe that social media will play an important part in connecting matrix organizations and teams in the future. If our objective is to cut across traditional silos and make cooperation and communication easy and inexpensive, then social media gives us an ideal tool for encouraging such behavior. It will make traditional hierarchies increasingly irrelevant.

In 2011, for the first time, companies spent more on internal applications of social media than on external ones. In marketing, social media has transformed communication with customers. People are more likely to trust the comments of others who are like them than the expensive broadcast adverts of producers. Now social media is poised to transform internal communication and ways of working.

Here are the top five ways I think social media can support matrix working.

Creating connections across silos

Social media tools like Twitter and Facebook encourage communication across traditional barriers. When you reach out and choose to follow people you are interested in, this tends to be irrespective of functional boundaries.

People will reach out across the organization and across the hierarchy to get solutions to their problems. They will pass comment and expect to be listened to. Companies will be unable to control the content of these conversations and internal communications will need to be able to respond quickly to trends and the issues that arise.

Those at the periphery of the organization, in customer service centers, or based in remote offices will find it much easier to join conversations and get their view across.

Sidestepping hierarchy

Social media tends to ignore traditional hierarchies. It encourages people to reach out and find someone with an answer, rather than just someone with a job title.

We choose to "follow" and pay attention to people we find interesting, well-informed, controversial, or entertaining. This will make a huge difference in internal communications. Who will we trust at a time of change? Will we pay attention to our departmental head or that well-informed, anonymous, and controversial Twitter commentator who has gained our trust with previous scoops and inside news?

There is a strong link between corporate culture and an organization's approach to social media use. If the instinct of the corporation is to control, then social media is usually not permitted or is closely controlled. In this case, social media is unlikely to work to the organization's benefit and could become highly disruptive.

One of the participants at the Tweet Camp raised an example of her government department, which allowed its employees to tweet, but only after approval. The approval process took approximately 12 days, which rather got in the way of social interaction.

The speed of conversations in the social space is so fast that we cannot expect to control them. We just have to join the conversation.

Making expertise visible

Social tools usually have profiles that are searchable. This will help us quickly identify experts and people with responsibility for specific decisions.

The specific objective of many matrix implementations is to share resources across traditional silos. Profile and search tools make this much easier. Once you have identified an expert, you can make instant and direct contact with a question or request.

Transforming the cost of cooperation

Social media can be used to assist in each of our four ways of working – teams, groups, communities, and networks.

It enables larger communities and networks to keep in touch at minimal cost. By making it easy to share and comment on information, social media creates the potential for cooperation to emerge.

It also enables "mass collaboration," such as the IBM Jam process, which allows all IBM employees and even external partners and customers to participate in large-scale debates. These have led to outcomes as diverse as updating the company's corporate values and collaborative product development.

Accelerated learning

Social media allows us to broaden our learning by connecting to people with similar jobs and challenges, both inside and outside our own organization.

In the past there were many barriers to cross-organizational learning. It was quite difficult to get approval for a site visit, or to share information. Today, when people have social networks in place across organizations, it is often easier for them to reach out and talk to an individual and get a response than to go through official channels.

Social elements will be introduced into a whole range of business processes so that people can quickly share their experiences and ideas about operating or improving a particular process.

As younger people who are used to being socially connected join the workforce, they will naturally use the familiar tools from their outside lives to do their work.

These trends will have big implications for the way we work together in organizations in the future. They will certainly encourage and enable more horizontal or matrix working.

Higher levels and lower costs of connection will also bring risks. Is everyone's opinion equally relevant? Will management become a popularity contest? What is public and what is private? It is going to be interesting!

Use the information in this chapter to make sure that you have the communications technology infrastructure in place to support the ways of working that you need in your team or organization. Ensure that your people are trained in the technologies they use and are skilled in creating participation and engagement in online communication. Consider experimenting with social media to see whether it helps connect your organization or team more effectively.

Before you leave this chapter

❏ Do you have the communications technologies in place to support the ways of working that you require?

❏ Are your teams, groups, communities, and networks using technology appropriately to support the way they work?

❏ Have people been trained in how to use these technologies?

❏ How much of your communication is directly relevant to the recipient?

❏ Do your people have the ability to create participation and engagement online?

❏ Have you started to experiment with social media to see what it can do for you?

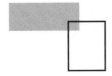

Part III
Control

In Part III I will focus on two particular challenges of control that are often mentioned by line managers – can we be accountable without control and how do we get things done without traditional authority? I will challenge these old paradigms and introduce some skills and tips for being effective in a matrix.

I will introduce a process for taking people through a series of systematic steps to ensure that they are capable and confident to perform, before moving on to a higher level of engagement, freedom, and autonomy at work.

I will also focus on the barriers to trust building in matrix teams and the steps we can take to build, maintain, and repair trust in this complex environment.

In Part III:

12

Accountability
without Control

A recipe for matrix success

Leaders who are new to a matrix often complain "I cannot be accountable for what I do not control," but in fact it is rare to have a match between accountability and control at work. Too much control at work may defeat the object of a matrix and may be an indication of poor performance.

In this chapter I will identify how to manage a planned imbalance between control and accountability, how to structure matrix roles and responsibilities based on this understanding, and how to build true accountability and engagement by giving individuals more freedom to choose their own commitments. The chapter covers:

❑ Hands up if you want to be punished – making accountability positive
❑ Span of control and span of accountability
❑ Horizontal and vertical accountabilities – managing them differently
❑ Choosing to commit

HANDS UP IF YOU WANT TO BE PUNISHED – MAKING ACCOUNTABILITY POSITIVE

Accountability is a concept in ethics and governance with several meanings. It is often used synonymously with such concepts as responsibility, answerability, blameworthiness, liability, and other terms associated with the expectation of account-giving. As an aspect of governance, it has been central to discussions related *to <u>problems</u> in the public sector, nonprofit and private (corporate) worlds. In leadership roles, accountability is the acknowledgment and assumption of responsibility for actions, products, decisions, and policies including the administration, governance, and implementation within the scope of the role or employment position and encompassing the obligation to <u>report, explain and be answerable for resulting consequences.</u>*

Wikipedia (my underlining for emphasis)

This is a typical definition of the word accountability. As you can see, it focuses largely on attributing responsibility or blame if something goes wrong. It calls us to account, to explain problems from the past and be answerable for the consequences. If this is our view of accountability, why would anyone raise their hands to be accountable?

Many industries are now subject to regulation to ensure accountability, often as a result of failures of trust in the past. Usually drafted by lawyers and politicians, these regulations and governance rules focus on senior levels of the organization and on top-down compliance. They are based on old-fashioned principles of command and control. They are backward looking and often designed to establish blame and sanctions retrospectively, or to prevent future idiocy. None of these is an effective principle for running a business.

The Vickers Report from the UK Independent Commission on banking consisted of 363 pages of recommendations and analysis on banking reform. It mentioned the word "loss" 536 times, about 1.5 times per page. It only talked about "profit" 30 times, once every 12 pages. The following words are not used anywhere in the document: autonomy, empowerment, celebration, learning, and people (except when referring to customers). The report does, however, make space for 23 mentions of control and 2 of sanctions.

Surely the real benefit of accountability is when it is forward looking, getting people engaged in creating a desired result? Where in this definition does it say we get to celebrate success, learn from our experiences, have a sense of ownership for the tasks, and enjoy the feeling of achievement when they succeed?

In our organization, as part of the kickoff of a major project or activity, we identify "who gets to celebrate" when we are successful. We do this to define the people who really have their "skin in the game" in advance. Otherwise, when we are successful, everyone celebrates and everyone claims a stake. It is nice and we want everyone to feel good about success, but this can dilute the recognition that should go to the people who really drove the thing forward. By defining them in advance, we keep focus on the real key contributors.

Project manager, specialty materials, USA

Success has many fathers, failure is an orphan.

English proverb

If accountability is continually equated with negative factors and blame, it is no wonder that people are reluctant to accept accountability over things they do not directly control.

A negative attitude to accountability has infected many individuals' view of their worlds. Normally when we hear the "no accountability without control" complaint it is a sign of one of three things:

❑ The leader is feeling out of control as a result of having to achieve results through influence and persuasion rather than through hierarchical authority.

❑ There is a lack of trust that others will play their part in delivering their areas of responsibility.

❑ The organization has a culture of blame and accountability brings risk along with it.

These are, of course, challenges for any individual. We often cannot change the organizational culture around us directly, but we can change and reframe the way we think about these issues. As leaders, we can also model the attitudes and behaviors that we want to encourage in our matrix.

My definition of accountability is: "A freely chosen commitment to own the responsibility for achieving a particular result."

Figure 12.1 Accountability

The matrix victim feels threatened and uncertain in the more ambiguous world of the matrix and takes refuge in complaints and resistance. They are waiting for someone else to solve problems for them and in a matrix they are often disappointed.

The matrix manager takes personal responsibility for solving their own problems, a behavior that we need to encourage in a matrix structure. It is part of developing the "matrix mindset." If we expect all issues to be escalated for resolution, then the organization will become very slow and expensive to run.

Matrix victims say	Matrix managers say
I cannot be accountable for what I cannot control	How can I work with others to get this done?
I do not have the resources	Where can I get the resources?
I was given this responsibility in my objectives	I chose to make this commitment and I will meet it

SPAN OF CONTROL AND
SPAN OF ACCOUNTABILITY

Robert Simons has studied the link between accountability and control. His research suggests that organizations consciously balance span of control (the resources over which an individual has direct control) and span of accountability (the results and performance outcomes for which they are held responsible) to achieve different outcomes.

If we think about the balance between span of accountability and span of control, there are only three options, and each of them drives a very different set of behaviors.

Accountabilities are smaller than the resources you control

In this case it is probable that you are underperforming or perhaps hoarding resources that could be used more effectively elsewhere. This is not a desirable situation.

People in 16 percent of companies in Simons' sample had a span of control that was greater than their span of accountability. All of these organizations were found to be underperforming, usually due to poor performance controls or excess resources.

Accountabilities equal your level of control

This situation can lead to efficiency: we are able simply to get on and do the work without relying on others. However, in a matrix work often crosses traditional vertical silos of function and geography and if each of us is only looking at our own narrow area, then we may miss critical issues that fall between the gaps.

Where span of accountability and span of control are equal, jobs can be performed by an individual focusing only on the resources they control. They do not need to take a broader perspective and will tend to concentrate on improving the efficiency of their own area of operation.

Accountabilities are broader than the resources you control

At first glance this may seem difficult to handle, but think about the behaviors that it requires. If people need to access resources that are outside their control, they need to think more broadly, seek out other resources, and work with others in order to be successful.

> *With span of accountability wider than span of control, an individual is accountable for figuring out how to turn opportunities into results even though he or she does not control the resources to get the job done.*
>
> "Accountability and control as catalysts for strategic exploration and exploitation," Harvard Business School working paper by Robert Simons

Where accountabilities are wider than the resources an individual controls, they have to reach out and explore opportunities to engage with others who control complementary resources to get things done.

These are precisely the behaviors that we want to encourage for breaking across the traditional silos in a matrix. It is therefore preferable in a matrix to design jobs where accountabilities routinely exceed control over resources.

Accountability > Control	Focus on exploring and collaboration
Accountability = Control	Focus on efficiency
Accountability < **Control**	Over-resourced or poor performance

Figure 12.2 Accountability and control

In 70 percent of the companies in Simons' research, there were jobs where the span of accountability was wider than the span of control. The more the companies in the study wanted to encourage exploration and entrepreneurship behaviors, the wider the gap.

We can use this thinking as a tool to encourage matrix behaviors:

❏ For those tasks where we want to focus on efficiency, we should try to balance accountability and control.
❏ For those tasks where we want to encourage a broader, more collaborative view across the organization, we should prefer accountabilities that are broader than the span of control.

When business processes and activities cut across traditional silos, accountabilities for end-to-end results will usually be broader than traditional job descriptions.

But, as always, be careful what you wish for.

We had a very competent group of directors in our business who were seen as potential general managers. To aid their development the vice presidents set up a Directors Council and gave them a broad brief to come up with ideas to improve the organization.

They started to grow into these broad accountabilities and came up with radical and wide-ranging ideas. They made proposals on strategy and major organization and business process changes. At this point the vice presidents started to get a bit nervous; this group was starting to supplant their areas of responsibility. The Directors Council was disbanded. Subsequently a number of the high-potential directors left the organization by their own choice.

HR director, business services, USA

In complex organizations, we depend on support functions and other individuals to play their parts in order to achieve success. Accountability will regularly be shared. In the more ambiguous and flexible structure of a matrix, narrowly drawn job descriptions will therefore be counterproductive.

Broader jobs bring higher levels of employee engagement by creating more meaningful work (with an end-to-end view of the impact of our work rather than a narrow silo perspective) and increased opportunities for learning and development.

HORIZONTAL AND VERTICAL ACCOUNTABILITIES – MANAGING THEM DIFFERENTLY

In a matrix, it is useful to manage vertical and horizontal accountabilities differently.

Vertical accountabilities can often be delivered by individuals completing their own functional work. In these areas, span of control may be more closely linked to span of accountability, to encourage the search for efficient solutions and to focus on the delivery of work that is within an individual's control.

However, most people in a matrix will also have horizontal accountabilities. Many activities are delivered by people collaborating across functions. In this case, accountabilities must be shared. It would make no sense for only the team or process or project leader to have accountability for the overall success of the activity.

Horizontal spans of accountability should be broader than spans of control to encourage people to take ownership of the whole process and to make sure that they do not "drop the ball" when moving between the traditional silos.

In matrix teams it is normal for team members to have a blend of individual and collective accountabilities.

In my objectives I am accountable for the overall delivery of the brand team plan. I share this accountability with the other core members of the team and the team lead.

I also have my personal goals to deliver certain functional work and specific tasks to the team. These are my individual accountabilities as a specialist. It is my job to make sure the two are aligned, as one cannot be successful without the other.

Market access manager, healthcare, Mexico

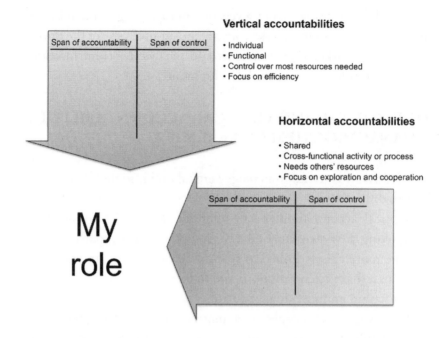

Vertical accountabilities

- Individual
- Functional
- Control over most resources needed
- Focus on efficiency

Horizontal accountabilities

- Shared
- Cross-functional activity or process
- Needs others' resources
- Focus on exploration and cooperation

Figure 12.3 My role

If it is routine in your organization for people to have complete control over all of the resources they need to deliver their accountabilities, then this may be an indication of performance problems. It will certainly drive behaviors and attitudes that can get in the way of successful matrix working.

CHOOSING TO COMMIT

People feel the highest levels of accountability and emotional engagement in their work when they choose their own commitments rather than having them given to them by others.

Instead of arguing that there is no accountability without control, perhaps it is more true to say that there is no accountability *with* control. If someone else is controlling your goals and role and tells you what your accountabilities are, then are you really committed? Where tasks are given rather than chosen, we should expect accountability to be weaker.

Because of this, we cannot really create true accountability unless we give up control to the individual to choose their own commitments. If you as the manager retain control, then you also retain accountability. The more you try to control people, the less accountable they become.

> *I have never had control and I never wanted it. If you create an environment where people truly participate, you do not need control. They know what needs to be done and they do it. And the more that people will devote themselves to your cause on a voluntary basis, a willing basis, the fewer hierarchies and control mechanisms you need. We are not looking for blind obedience. We are looking for people who, on their own initiative, want to be doing what they are doing, because they consider it to be a worthy objective.*
>
> Herb Kelleher, former CEO, Southwest Airlines

Use the information in this chapter to make sure that your span of accountability and control is appropriate to your role and to the matrix behaviors and mindset that you want to encourage.

In Chapter 14 I will introduce a continuous improvement process for building capability and relaxing control, with the objective of moving accountability further into the hands of our people and creating even higher levels of engagement.

If you want to read more on accountability and control, try *Accountability: Freedom and Responsibility without Control* by Rob Lebow and Randy Spitzer, or *The Oz Principle: Getting Results through Individual and Organizational Accountability* by Roger Connors, Tom Smith, and Craig R Hickman.

Before you leave this chapter

❑ Do accountabilities in your business look forward and focus on recognition, celebration, learning, and motivation, or are they about the past and focus on blame or fear of failure?
❑ What is the balance between span of control and span of accountability in your goals?

❏ Does the balance of span of control and accountability in your vertical and horizontal goals make sense for your role and support matrix working behaviors?

❏ How can you give your people more opportunity to choose their commitments rather than having them set by managers?

13

Power and Influence
without Authority

We are all big dogs now

The same managers who claim that they can only be accountable for things they do not control are often also concerned about the need to get things done through influence rather than traditional authority.

In reality, talented managers have always used a wide range of influence techniques and sources of power to get things done. Too much reliance on authority can damage engagement and create resistance.

In this chapter I will identify the sources of power and influence to which we have access and suggest how to apply them in a matrix to get things done. The chapter covers:

❏ More than just authority
❏ Sources and consequences of power in the matrix
❏ The five steps to influence
❏ Multiple bosses – two's company, three's a matrix
❏ Staying visible when working remotely

MORE THAN JUST AUTHORITY

I went to a meeting as a newly promoted executive and, when there was a disagreement, I raised my voice and started laying down the law. Another senior executive took me to one side and explained, "In your career up to now you were the big dog: when you barked the others jumped. Now you are an executive who will be working with peers of equal power. We are all big dogs now and barking just will not get it done."

It was strange that the more I got promoted, the less that traditional power and hierarchy helped me to get things done and the more I had to create alliances and influence people at senior levels.

Newly promoted executive, energy, France

In many organizations you can make good progress in your early career by using positional power and traditional authority to get things done. Junior managers often have clear areas of responsibility and accountability and are able to deliver many of their key objectives and metrics by focusing on their own area of responsibility. Within that area, they are indeed a "big dog" and can use that power to get things done quite effectively.

However, once we are promoted to executive level in our organization, or when we start working in a more ambiguous matrix role where our span of accountability is broader than our span of control, we find that there is a much greater need to work across traditional organizational boundaries. We need to build alliances and influence people we do not have formal authority over. We have to learn to engage peers or superiors who are just as positionally powerful as we are and individual experts we rely on for success.

We have to find other skills and means of getting things done. Individuals who cling too long to legacy hierarchical and positional power often do not survive the transition to senior levels in complex organizations.

The more talented senior leaders have always used a broader range of skills and ways of getting things done and are able to adapt more easily to this new environment. Senior leaders have worked in this networked way for a long time, and we put a huge amount of time and expense into helping them develop strong networks and relationships. We invest in making sure that these people are well informed, networked, and empowered, and members of this group typically spend much time together discussing strategy at conferences and leadership retreats.

In a matrix, we are asking people much further down in the organization to let go of positional and hierarchical power and get much more done through influence, networks, and expertise. In effect, we are asking them to behave in the way senior leaders always have. We are asking them to become "big dogs" too.

For them to do this successfully, we need to make sure that they have the skills, information, confidence, time, and backing to operate in this way. Otherwise, we should not be surprised if they fall back on traditional forms of power, which may be much less effective at getting things done in the matrix.

SOURCES AND CONSEQUENCES OF POWER IN THE MATRIX

One of the reasons we set up a matrix is to balance the power of traditional silos by adding more horizontal reporting lines. Hierarchical control and power may be shared or absent in a matrix, so getting things done involves exercising a wider range of sources of power and influence.

It is also important to understand the likely consequences if you utilize these different forms of power.

Every action creates an opposite and equal reaction.
Newton's third law of motion

Here is a brief summary of the 12 most common types of power to which you may have access, as well as the consequences of using them.

❏ **Coercive** – the use or threat of force has become less effective in organizations. It still exists at some level, such as in terminating the employment of poor performers. However, it tends to create unwilling compliance and the level of resistance means that its use is nearly always counterproductive in getting things done.

❏ **Normative** – based on values. This is an extremely important source of power in a matrix. It provides guidance on the right way to resolve complex dilemmas and choices across complex reporting lines, geographies, and cultures. Matrix organizations require strong shared practices and beliefs to be successful.

❏ **Personal** – respect for your individual characteristics. This remains important in a matrix, but it relies on your degree of visibility in the organization. People need great networks and good communication skills to be successful at transmitting their personal power across the organization.

❏ **Expert** – from superior knowledge, skills, and abilities. One of the objectives of a matrix is to give easier access to expertise. Expertise is extremely powerful in a matrix and we need mechanisms to make it simple to identify and access. Social media profiles will make it easier in the future to find and contact individual experts without going through the whole organization.

❏ **Position** – the power of role. In a matrix, positional power is often shared and therefore may be diluted. Managers need to find ways to align and ally with their colleagues. The use of traditional hierarchical authority as a source of power is likely to be less productive in creating accountability, engagement, and responsibility.

❏ **Reward** – the ability to deliver rewards and punishments. In a matrix this will be shared and may be subject to input from peers and colleagues across the organization, rather than being entirely within the hands of the line manager. Financial rewards are rather blunt tools for encouraging cooperation. Recognition and other more immediate forms of reward become more powerful.

❏ **Relationship** – the power of trust, shared goals, and a sense of identification. This is extremely important; relationships will increasingly cross the organization rather than being vested in vertical functions. This form of power tends to create a willing style of followership.

❏ **Information** – having more and better sources of information. While this can be powerful, it should be our objective in a matrix to make information visible and transparent to everyone involved in the process or activity. If individuals are hoarding information in order to create power for themselves, this is counterproductive.

❏ **Resources** – this power may be at an organizational level, or it could be simply an individual's ability to decide how they spend their time. One goal of introducing a matrix is to share resources more freely across the organization. Using resources politically to increase your power may not be welcome.

❏ **Alliances** – we can derive power from the people we know and are able to influence and from the other people we can bring with us once we are persuaded. Alliances are an important source of influence and power in the matrix.

❏ **Social influence** – who trusts our opinion and listens to what we say? This type of influence is being magnified by social media, as individuals develop a "followership" of people who choose to pay attention to them.

❏ **Reciprocity** – the power of having a favor in the bank. People seek ways to repay those who have helped them in the past. It is always useful to find opportunities to give support in advance, so that support is available in return when you need it.

Traditional, command-and-control forms of power, such as position, hierarchy, and coercion, become less and less effective among well-educated and skilled employees. At best, they may create an unwilling style of followership where compliance is more important than genuine commitment. In general, even if you have access to these forms of power, they should be used very sparingly.

Other forms of power such as normative, expertise, relationship, and social influence are becoming increasingly important in a matrix. The use of these types of power is likely to create a more positive form of employee engagement.

> *We created this matrix organization so that any individual could reach out and access any other individual who could help them with a problem. Not so that they have to talk to every person in between.*
>
> R&D associate, specialist materials, USA

THE FIVE STEPS TO INFLUENCE

The skill of influencing is essential in a matrix, where we cannot use traditional authority and power to get things done. Influencing is a skill that is very simple in principle but can be very difficult in practice.

Planned influencing consists of five steps:

1. Being clear about what you are trying to achieve.
2. Identifying the individuals you need to influence to get there.
3. Understanding what they value.
4. Identifying the "currencies" available to influence them.
5. Taking actions based on this knowledge to achieve your goals.

There are some particular challenges in applying some of these steps in a matrix environment.

Being clear about what you are trying to achieve

If you are not clear what your goal is, you are unlikely to be successful. It is good practice to write your influencing goals down and to think through any subgoals, barriers, and measurements of success.

There is an important mindset issue here as well. Treat each individual as if they will want to cooperate, as potential allies in the task, rather than starting with an adversarial view that you have to persuade someone to do something against their will.

Identifying the individuals you need to influence to get there

This can be more complex in a matrix, as you may need to influence people you do not know, who are in different locations or from different cultures. Identify the people whose help you need to achieve your goals and do some analysis on what you already know about them.

Understanding what they value

The essence of influence without authority is exchange: what I can offer you in exchange for your cooperation and your attention. The essence of exchange is to understand your "currencies."

Currency in this sense is a technical term meaning anything that the individual values. The biggest mistake in influence is to offer things that *you* value rather than things that the individual you are trying to influence values. A currency only has the value attributed to it by the recipient.

A colleague of mine was trying to persuade me to help with a virtual team project. He was very excited that the project would offer more opportunities for travel. For him that was great, because he rarely traveled and he was looking forward to the variety. I already travel too much, so the chance to take an additional business trip was a real turnoff for me.

L&D manager, consulting, UK

In a matrix we are often trying to influence people we do not know well. Many of Global Integration's clients invest in interpersonal skills training, which equips participants with a model to understand their own behavior and that of others. Such models can be extremely useful in understanding the relationship between individuals and what the people you are trying to influence may value.

In our workshops we sometimes use the Strength Deployment Inventory® (SDI) from Personal Strengths. This helps you to identify your style under normal conditions and when in conflict, and offers a very simple framework for analyzing the preferences of others and how people are likely to perceive each other. We use it because it is simple, graphical, and the questionnaires have been translated into a wide range of languages.

Cross-cultural and interpersonal skills training is an important component of our ability to be successful in a global matrix. It helps us to understand the groups and individuals we may be trying to influence. We need a nonjudgmental language for talking about and analyzing other people's styles.

You may also find it useful to discover anything you can about the goals of the person you are trying to influence, their concerns, how these are measured, and their view of the world. You can do this directly or by talking to other people who know them. However, be careful not to take this too far or it may appear manipulative, or worse.

I met with a supplier recently and they had obviously done their homework. They understood my goals and our organization pretty well. Then they dropped in some information about previous companies I had worked for and it was clear that they had looked at my LinkedIn profile. Further into the conversation, however, they referred to a couple of personal interests that probably came from my Facebook profile. Now it started to feel intrusive and even creepy.

Purchasing manager, software, USA

Sometimes the simplest approach to finding out what people value is to ask: "What do you want to get out of this?"

I was working with a new colleague on a virtual project and I wanted to understand what was in it for them. I didn't really know them, so I just called them up. I told them I was looking forward to working with them and that I appreciated that this would be extra work for them. I asked, "Is there anything in particular you would like to get out of this experience?" They told me that they thought it was a good opportunity to build their network internationally, so I was able to help them do that as part of the project.

Project manager, luxury goods, China

In the worst case, at least you know what you are working with.

I asked a new member of the team what they wanted to get out of working on this team. They told me there was nothing, "it is just extra work and I want to get it out of the way as quickly as possible." Initially I was a bit taken aback, but strangely, this was helpful as I was able to work with them to put together a plan to get their part of the activity done as quickly and simply as possible – which was my objective too.

Virtual team leader, aerospace, UK

Identifying the "currencies" available to influence them

Once you understand the currencies that this individual values, you can look for opportunities to build these into the team, project, or activity.

Let me be clear, I am not talking about identifying currencies for every little thing. We should expect cooperation from our colleagues just because we are part of the same organization. Also, we should recognize that not everything is a benefit; sometimes boring work just needs to be done. But if we want an individual to go "above and beyond" or to increase their motivation to cooperate, why not find out what is in it for them and see whether you can help?

If you think creatively, you will always be able to find currencies that you can use to influence others. Here are some that our workshop participants often identify:

❏ **Variety** – the chance to do something new.
❏ **Exposure** – the chance to be seen by other people who might be useful to their future career.
❏ **Networking** – the chance to build a network and contacts in new areas.
❏ **Travel** – for those who do not travel often this can be very motivating.
❏ **Personal development** – to learn new skills or technologies.
❏ **Favors or goodwill** – it is often useful to have a favor "in the bank" for when one is needed in the future.
❏ **Values** – appealing to someone to do the right thing for the customer or the business.
❏ **Reputation** – it is nice to be sought out and even nicer to be recognized.

With a little thought and creativity, you will find a whole range of currencies you have access to. A good place to look is to think about what the individual is not getting in their current role. If their boss never gives feedback, for example, the opportunity to receive good-quality feedback might be valuable.

But remember that a currency only has the value that the recipient puts on it. Make sure that you find out and offer what the recipient values, not what *you* think is valuable.

The simplest way to find out what people value is to ask.

You may find other ideas on currencies and influencing strategies by analyzing your sources of power, listed earlier in this chapter.

Taking action based on this knowledge to achieve your goals

In a matrix you will often be extending your powers of influence through technology and to diverse people in multiple locations.

Remember that everything you do is a carrier of communication about *you*. The way you respond to an email, how you make yourself available to help, and your style all carry important information about your willingness to cooperate and will influence others' willingness to cooperate with you.

Working in a matrix requires relatively high levels of interdependence. People need to work together to access resources and are often dealing with complex problems that require a number of different perspectives. In this environment cooperation makes more sense than in one in which you have complete control over your resources, and where interdependence is lower.

There is some evidence that organizations are more political when resources can be controlled more closely, so a matrix may in fact help make an organization less political.

MULTIPLE BOSSES – TWO'S COMPANY, THREE'S A MATRIX

The defining characteristic of a matrix organizational structure is the existence of more than one boss. This violates the traditional management principles of unity of command and a single point of accountability, which can no longer cope with the complexity of modern organizations.

In a complex organization, individuals may have several solid- or dotted-line bosses and a number of key stakeholders who, despite having no formal reporting line, have a big influence on that individual.

In this section we will look at the example of an individual who has a single solid-line report and a dotted line to a virtual team leader. I have chosen this because this tends to be one of the more challenging situations to manage.

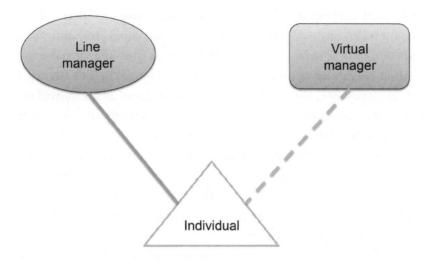

Figure 13.1   Multiple bosses

You can apply the same principles to a multiple solid-line reporting situation. In this kind of relationship, power and influence change for everyone concerned.

The line manager

Line managers used to have sole control over the traditional management tools. They set objectives and measures, conducted performance appraisals, recommended rewards, and discussed development plans and careers.

These are all powerful tools to get an individual to do what you want. Nevertheless, even with these tools it can sometimes be hard to influence your direct reports.

The solid-line manager still has access to traditional sources of power such as authority, hierarchy, position, and even coercion. However, these sources of power become less effective with skilled and empowered people and their use may undermine engagement and be increasingly counterproductive.

The line manager in a matrix now has to spend much more time and effort getting aligned with their virtual manager peers. They need to take into account virtual team goals, measures, and other requirements in their planning and get input from the virtual manager on performance and development issues. For the line manager this is extra work, usually for little benefit to them as an individual. Direct-line managers often feel that their authority and access to resources have been undermined by the matrix.

The solid-line manager usually maintains responsibility for driving the key people-management processes such as goal setting and reward, but is required to get input from the virtual team manager. If there are two solid-line relationships then one of them will often be designated as a "host manager."

Host managers are responsible for the individual's communication and development needs and will often, although not always, be associated with the physical location where the individual is based.

If the solid reporting line is to the function, then the line manager will also be responsible for functional development and the "vertical" goals that flow down the functional reporting lines.

Three critical issues on which the line manager and virtual manager need to stay in contact are:

❑ **Escalation** – if the individual is finding it difficult to resolve issues, they will escalate them up one or both of the reporting lines. The managers involved must present a consistent response to these escalations, preferably by insisting that they are to both of them.
❑ **Alignment** – the line and virtual managers need to stay aligned in their communication messages to the individual and during goal-setting, appraisal, and performance-management processes.
❑ **Prioritization** – if the individual has resource limitation issues, then line and virtual managers need either to give assistance on prioritization of tasks and time or to empower the individual to do this and support their decisions.

If the line and virtual manager are not sufficiently aligned in these areas, individuals will usually learn to make such decisions for themselves.

My two bosses are not well aligned. If I take priority problems to them each of them tells me that their leg of the matrix takes priority. That doesn't help me.

You can only escalate so much. If you escalate constantly it makes you look incompetent, so at the end of the day I have learned to solve the problem for myself. It is usually easier to ask for forgiveness than permission.

Marketing associate, industrials, USA

This works well with capable and confident people, but can cause poor judgment calls or unnecessary stress for individuals who do not have the skills to manage such a situation.

The virtual team manager

A virtual team manager can "hijack" some of the traditional tools of management by aligning closely with the line manager. If the virtual team goals are written into the individual's formal objectives, then the goal-setting and performance-management system will reinforce the virtual team goals, too.

However, even if the direct line manager agrees to a formal commitment of, say, 20 percent of the individual's time, this is not the end of the job. Most people in complex organizations are already busy.

My boss called me to tell me that he had agreed that I could spend 10 percent of my time on this new virtual project. I explained that I was already overloaded and asked which 10 percent of my existing workload I could stop doing to make space for it. He just laughed.

IT manager, chemicals, USA

The virtual team manager also needs to engage directly with the individual to gain their commitment. Because people are busy and have competing demands on their time, it is the employees who will decide how much time the virtual team really gets.

The virtual manager and the line manager can find themselves competing for attention and mind share. It is important that they are aligned to keep this on a positive footing, otherwise they may find themselves being played off against each other.

The virtual team manager is often responsible for driving a specific project or cross-functional activity. In this capacity they are usually responsible for any development and training required that is specific to the activity.

In a matrix, where the individual is spending most of their time on horizontal activity such as a cross-functional project or process and the vertical reporting line is mainly functional, then the virtual team manager may direct most of an individual's activity. In that case, a much larger proportion of the performance-management information should lie with the virtual team leader.

The virtual team manager does have some power through their role and through the agreement with the line manager, but for much of the time they are effectively in an "influence without authority" situation. It is therefore essential for them to understand their sources of power and currencies of influence.

The virtual team manager needs to use a much wider range of skills and elements to attract the individual's motivation and cooperation, and this can lead to increased engagement and satisfaction among team members.

We asked people about their satisfaction with their line managers (solid line) and their virtual team managers (dotted line). We were surprised to find that people were slightly more satisfied with their virtual team managers. When we asked why, people told us that their virtual team managers tried harder and used a wider range of techniques to keep them engaged and motivated, whereas the direct line manager more often fell back on telling them what to do.

Climate survey manager, telecoms, UK

The individual

The man with two masters is a free man.

Anon

You might think that an individual with two bosses would receive more supervision and input. In reality, skilled individuals in the matrix actually make their own decisions on prioritization and how they should spend their time. At any one time, each of your matrix bosses may only have half of the picture. If you have two or more bosses, it is your job to make sure that they are fully informed and aligned, otherwise the problem can become yours.

Individuals in a matrix need to be much more self-managing. They have to be alert to inconsistencies and alignment issues. As an individual, you need to manage your multiple bosses and their perceptions of you so that you can be successful.

People from different functions and activities can have very different views of the world. They have studied for different qualifications, they are rewarded for different actions, they receive different information, and they focus on the things that are relevant to their own roles. For this reason, the vertical and horizontal worlds of your bosses may be quite different. The only point at which they may come together is in your goals and the way you are managed.

If you want to be empowered, you need to create confidence in your leaders to let you go and leave you alone to do your job.

Because these tradeoff and prioritization decisions are, in practice, made by individuals further down in the organization, managers need to make sure that these individuals have the information, skills, and authority to manage them effectively.

If this does not happen, individuals will often prioritize on the basis of what *they* think is important, or what they enjoy or find most personally beneficial.

Each individual has access to their own sources of power, including expertise and resource-allocation power (their own time).

Strong currencies for the individual to use upward include reliability, keeping the boss informed (no surprises), loyalty, exceeding expectations, providing support, and coming up with new ideas and suggestions.

As an individual in the matrix, do not expect too much from your leaders. They may only have half the picture of your total role and a fraction of the motivation that you should have to solve your own problems. This can be good news for engagement: it gives you the opportunity to carve out higher levels of ownership and autonomy in your own role! A mature relationship between all three parties is likely to be more successful than an unbalanced one in which the individual is waiting for direction from two more senior people.

STAYING VISIBLE WHEN WORKING REMOTELY

Global Integration's online survey of over 4,000 people identified one of the top three concerns for individuals in matrix and virtual teams as: "How do I stay visible when working remotely?"

Visibility is important for individuals in a matrix. Visibility helps them in developing their network and in future career development. It is also important for teams and departments, because visibility helps them get access to attention and resources for their activities, to maintain priorities, and to attract good people to want to work with them.

In large companies, especially where people are working in a virtual team away from the center of power, there is a real risk of "out of sight, out of mind." It is not enough to do a good job; you also need to be visible.

Some of our participants, especially the engineers, argue that it should not be this way; doing good work should be enough. Part of me agrees in principle, but the reality is that in large, complex organizations perception is important; performance is not enough on its own.

I am definitely not encouraging you to become one of the slick corporate politicians who spend more time "spinning" a good message than doing a good job. If, however, you are working remotely or in a virtual team, you do need to manage your visibility.

I am assuming that you are already doing a good job, but one point of warning: if you are a terrible performer, you should definitely not work on your visibility!

A framework that some organizations employ for thinking about visibility is PIE, which stands for the three key elements of visibility in virtual teams:

❏ **Performance** – what you achieve.
❏ **Image** – the picture of yourself that you project.
❏ **Exposure** – who knows about you.

This process has been used extensively by organizations such as GE in identifying how individuals become perceived as having high potential. All three of the factors are important and need to be managed.

When we give this model to participants in our workshops and ask them to estimate how much each of these factors contributes to perception in their organizations, we get a range of responses. In most cases they agree that exposure is the most important of the three:

❏ Performance = 10–45%
❏ Image = 15–25%
❏ Exposure = 30–40%

Most participants feel that performance should count for more in their company, but concede that in reality it probably does not. My own view is that performance is a precondition or an entry ticket to the game. If you are not performing, then image and exposure will only be harmful.

It is clear that performance alone is not sufficient to create visibility in a large, complex organization. Most people spend nearly all of their time on performance; while this is how it should be, if you are not spending any time at all on managing your image and exposure, you may be missing an opportunity.

Repeated exposure to the right people helps enormously in career development. If you are a known quantity, your name comes up in promotion discussions; people tend to prefer the familiar because it reduces uncertainty. This is why people who stay close to the center of power have traditionally been promoted more quickly than those who work at the periphery.

This is a particular challenge today when individuals are spread around the world. Organizations need to make sure that their best talent is visible as well as capable.

In my organization, when a senior leader visits a site they typically have dinner or lunch with a group of high potentials who are based there. It helps the individuals to be visible and it helps the senior leader to get a different perspective on the business from people who typically have a position further down the organization than those they came to visit.

HR business partner, engineering, USA

You probably have a network of people who are important to your career. It may be worth creating a network map, with the purpose of advancing your career and identifying the key stakeholders you need to stay visible to. Think about the currencies and influencing tools you have to create a good impression with these people and always have a plan of what you want to achieve.

You can get useful information about what works in your corporate culture by spotting the people who are already successful. What is it that they do that makes them successful? How do they exercise influence and power in a culturally appropriate way?

Pay particular attention to those who exercise a level of influence that is disproportionate to their position in the hierarchy – they are probably the experts at doing this.

The exercise of power and influence is an important lever to success in any organization. In a matrix, exercising influence is more complex because we are working with a more diverse group of people when we often do not know them very well. We also have to apply the skills of influence across distance, national and functional cultural differences, time zones, and through the medium of communications technology.

The reduction in effectiveness of traditional types of power and authority means that managers need to become more sophisticated and influential in the approaches they use to get things done. If successful, this can lead to higher levels of employee engagement.

Use the information in this chapter to be more purposeful and systematic in the way you exercise influence. It is a critical skill in matrix working.

If you want to read more on this topic, try *Influence without Authority* by Alan R Cohen and David L Bradford.

Before you leave this chapter

❏ What sources of power and influence do you have access to in the matrix?

❏ Are they the right ones to get things done?

❏ Choose an important issue on which you are trying to influence others. Are you clear about each of the five steps?
- Be clear about what you are trying to achieve.
- Identify the individuals you need to influence to get there.
- Understand what they value.
- Identify the "currencies" that you have to influence them.
- Take actions based on this knowledge to achieve your goals.

❏ Are the roles of multiple bosses and the individuals who report to them clear in your organization?

❏ Do you and your team or organization have sufficient visibility to enable you to be successful?

14

From Empowerment to Freedom

Continuous improvement for people

Anyone who has had any management education in the last 30 years knows that empowerment is a good thing – it builds engagement and productivity and develops and retains good people.

But in real life sometimes we are under pressure: we do not have the time or budget we would like, or we lack confidence that others will play their part. We are skilled and hard-working and it is just quicker to do something ourselves than to delegate the task.

In a matrix we are often working with strangers and relying on resources that we do not control. In this complex environment, it can feel more risky to empower. What we need in the words of one of our clients is "a controlled process for giving empowerment."

In this chapter I will introduce a managed process for building capability, confidence, and the right level of support for our people. I will then propose a more radical step of giving people "empowerment by right." The chapter covers:

❏ Building capability
❏ Establishing mutual confidence
❏ Agreeing new support levels
❏ Moving beyond empowerment to freedom

In working with thousands of managers in matrix and virtual teams, Global Integration has developed a simple four-stage process for making sure that we are continuously empowering people without abandoning them.

This is a great company and right from the start they gave me a tremendous amount of trust to get on and do things. At the beginning this was actually quite uncomfortable. There was very little structure and I would have appreciated a bit more direction in the early stages. Now I am more experienced and I really enjoy the freedom, but it was a tough learning curve.

Marketing manager, IT services, Egypt

BUILDING CAPABILITY

When an individual is new to the team or organization, our focus should be on helping them build the capability to do the job.

It is foolish and unfair to empower people who are not capable of performing their job. We need first to make sure that they get the training, information, and tools to develop this capability.

Most organizations have some form of capability-building process, particularly for developing the technical skills required. In Chapter 16 I will make some recommendations on the capabilities required for leaders, team members, and individuals to be successful in a matrix environment.

During this initial phase we should expect a fair amount of contact and escalation from the individual, who will want to ask questions and to discuss options. Escalations are an important source of information on capability.

When I moved into manufacturing, I took over from a predecessor who wanted to know what was going on in detail. It was a 24-hours-a-day, seven-days-a-week operation, so I got many telephone calls in the evenings and weekends from my production managers.

At the same time I was undergoing quality training and learning that, if there was a problem with a product, my job was to fix the problem and then fix the process so that it couldn't happen again – the essence of continuous improvement.

I started to see the phone calls as indications that my managers were not capable of solving problems for themselves. I made a note of the reasons for the calls and categorized the issues behind them. I organized training and updated the documentation they had access to.

Once I was confident that they had the capability, I refused to answer their questions on the phone; instead, I referred them to the relevant training or documentation or coached them on their views of what they should do. They quickly realized that they could solve these problems for themselves and the number of calls reduced radically.

Keep a record of what kinds of issues are escalated to you by your people. What knowledge, skills, information, or authority would they need to solve this problem for themselves next time?

You can use a similar approach with issues that you escalate to your boss.

I went along to my boss to discuss some issues, but before I did so I prepared my own thoughts. As we talked through the issues, I asked if I could get some training or have access to information or levels of authority that would mean I didn't need to bother him with that issue in the future. In one case, he said no, there were some things he wanted to retain authority to deal with himself; but in most cases he was happy to let me take on more responsibility – it made his job easier, too.

HR business partner, media, UK

Make a note of which issues you escalate upward. What knowledge, skills, information, or authority would you need to be able to solve this problem for yourself next time?

Once an individual is capable of doing the job, we move on to the next phase, which is about mutual confidence.

ESTABLISHING MUTUAL CONFIDENCE

In this phase, the individual is capable of doing the job but may not be moving on to take greater levels of autonomy and responsibility for how it is performed. This may be because they lack confidence or are unwilling to take on more, or it may be that you lack the confidence to let them go.

This phase is all about mutual confidence. We only empower people when we trust them and are confident of their ability, and people only take responsibility when they are confident that they can succeed and be supported.

Your confidence in them

As managers, we should always start by looking at ourselves.

When I was learning to be a trainer, I was coached by a very experienced facilitator. I was finding one of my early workshops difficult, the participants were not very responsive, and I remarked to him that it was "like pulling teeth" getting them to do anything. My coach responded: "If a workshop ever feels like you are pulling teeth, ask what you have done to create a dentist's chair."

When we take on a new job, we inherit the leadership style and practices of our predecessor. For a maximum of 12 months we can use that as an excuse. After that, leaders get the followers they deserve.

Nobody sets out to be a micromanager. However, there are some common micromanagement traps that can lead us to apply a higher level of control than is really necessary. We can fall into these traps from the best intentions, or we may inherit a situation where a high level of control has become embedded in the way of working.

Recognizing and avoiding these traps are essential to empowerment and for you to avoid becoming an "accidental micromanager."

I worked in a technical problem-solving role. I enjoyed problem solving and I was good at it, so good in fact that I got promoted to manage the department. When problems came up, my first instinct was to solve them myself. Because I was more experienced than most people in the team, I could usually do it faster and thought it was helpful to give people solutions as quickly as possible.

It took me a while to realize that people were bringing me problems without bothering to think them through for themselves. They knew I would just give them a solution. Because people constantly came to me with their problems, I also started to doubt their capability, so I started to keep a closer eye on their work. Before long I became a micromanager. I was only trying to help.

IT manager, software, India

Hard-working, enthusiastic people, particularly those who have come up through a technical problem-solving route, love to solve problems and be helpful. This can easily lead them to take on responsibility for too much and disempower their people, despite their good intentions.

Three common micromanagement traps are:

❏ **Focusing on problem solving rather than people development.** As an experienced person it is often faster to solve problems yourself, but this doesn't allow your people to grow.

❏ **Not having confidence in your people to execute effectively.** In a matrix we are often dependent on people we do not know well to achieve our own goals. It is tough to empower those we may rarely meet.

❏ **Having too a high a need for personal control.** Individuals differ widely on the amount of control with which they feel comfortable. Mismatches between personal control needs can cause frustration between managers and their people.

How would you rate yourself against these three key micromanagement traps? Try filling in the grid on the next page.

If you recognize these factors "sometimes" or "often," this may be a sign that your management style could lead to higher levels of control than are really necessary. These are easy traps to fall into and it is always a matter of balance, as too little involvement can be a problem as well.

A great question to ask is: "Does it need to be me?" If it does need to be you that makes this decision or solves this problem, then ask: "Why does it need to be me?" Perhaps you have not developed the capability or confidence of others in your team to solve these problems or make these decisions.

Micromanagement undermines many of the drivers of employee engagement by making work more frustrating, reducing trust and autonomy, preventing learning, and damaging relationships.

If you are a manager, always start by focusing on yourself and on any barriers to letting go.

	Rarely	Some-times	Often
FOCUSING ON PROBLEM SOLVING RATHER THAN PEOPLE DEVELOPMENT			
I find it quicker to do things myself when I am busy, rather than get my people involved			
I tend to give solutions to problems rather than use an "ask" style of coaching			
NOT HAVING CONFIDENCE IN YOUR PEOPLE TO EXECUTE EFFECTIVELY			
I want to stay involved with problems my people are dealing with to make sure everything is handled correctly			
I am not sure my people have the capability needed to perform their jobs fully			
HAVING TOO A HIGH A NEED FOR PERSONAL CONTROL			
I feel uncomfortable if I do not know everything that is going on in my area of responsibility			
I think managers should know more than their people do about how to do their jobs			

In a matrix there are additional factors that may undermine our confidence in our people. A wide range of factors can create misunderstanding or doubt. Cultural differences, communicating through technology, infrequent face-to-face contact, and competing goals can all undermine trust and confidence. In the next chapter I will look specifically at building trust in this complex environment, as this is an essential component in developing confidence and empowerment.

Giving feedback to a manager who is micromanaging you can be challenging. You can track your escalations to give you some ideas and great opportunities for when to push back. If your relationship is good, you can be more explicit about the level of control you are experiencing, how it makes you feel, and where you think there is the potential to relax the level of control.

Participants on our workshops are often extremely frustrated by bosses who micromanage them. My advice is that they have three choices: change it, live with it, or leave it. It is relatively hard to change your boss (though you should definitely try). I do not usually recommend living with it for an extended period, as this can damage your development. So if all else fails, look for a new boss.

But do not forget also to look at yourself – what have *you* done to give your bosses the confidence to give you more autonomy?

Their confidence in themselves

If you are confident to let the individual go but they are not taking on responsibility for themselves, then you need to help them manage the transition.

The first step is to clarify your expectations. People may be referring problems to you because it is a pattern that you or a previous manager has encouraged, or it might have been the appropriate style when they were new to the role.

This is the time to push back gently and explain that you expect people to have a higher level of autonomy and solve problems for themselves. This may be all it takes to start someone on the journey to higher levels of empowerment.

If individuals continue to involve you in issues that you think they already have the capability to deal with themselves, then the tool to use is nondirective coaching.

In nondirective coaching you ask the individual questions to help them to think through the problem and come up with their own solutions. In this style of coaching you do not tell people the answer or even give them ideas and suggestions. If you do, you take back ownership of the process and the problem and take accountability away from the individual.

By asking open questions and guiding the coachee through a process that takes them from clarifying their purpose, through to identifying options, plans, and their commitment to act, you are helping them to understand that they are able to solve the problem for themselves. People are also much more committed to their own ideas than to those that other people give them.

Nondirective coaching is very simple in principle. You ask open questions (in English, open questions usually begin with the words what, why, when, where, and how) in a simple, five-stage process:

❏ **Purpose** – What is the purpose of the coaching? What outcome are you looking for?
❏ **History** – What have you tried so far? What worked? What didn't? Why?
❏ **Options** – What else could you do?
❏ **Next steps** – How will you implement this idea? What barriers do you see to getting this done? How will you overcome them?
❏ **Exit** – What other help do you need?

Nondirective coaching is a very powerful technique. The vast majority of managers, however, really struggle with only asking questions and not giving ideas and solutions. It is a big learning experience for them to practice this technique in our workshops, and to realize how strongly their natural style is to jump into solving problems rather than coaching.

In contrast, individuals normally enjoy being coached: they come up with their own solutions and find it helpful to be listened to by someone who doesn't have an agenda or a point of view to push.

This style of coaching is extremely useful in building mutual confidence. The individual learns that they can solve the problem for themselves and the manager has the opportunity to listen to their thinking and make sure that they have not missed anything critical.

The best coaching is carried out in an environment of trust. However, it can also be used to push back to individuals who are repeatedly escalating issues unnecessarily. In this case, once an individual asks for help, the manager initiates the coaching by saying: "I think you already know the answer to that, so let me coach you through it."

If individuals are unwilling to take on responsibility, they will feel uncomfortable with this style of coaching. As a manager, you then have to judge whether it is really a lack of capability (in which case they need more training or information) or a lack of willingness to take on responsibility.

In either case, your objective is to develop the individual to a state where they are capable and confident in doing their job and only seek your involvement when they need support.

This is essential in a matrix organization, where you may be operating across time zones, cultural differences, and multiple locations. If individuals cannot solve problems for themselves and require your input, you are likely to become a bottleneck and you will need to be accessible 24/7 to solve problems.

AGREEING NEW SUPPORT LEVELS

At this stage, you have built a high level of capability and mutual confidence in your people's ability to operate. This is your opportunity to relax any controls you have in place and to agree new, lower levels of control.

If you build more capable and confident people but do not relax your controls and let them take on more responsibility, then eventually you will create frustration. People will be bumping up against a ceiling of control.

Schedule a review meeting with the individual. Ask them to consider the factors below and meet to create a shared expectation for the future.

❑ **What support levels do we expect of each other?** How often will we meet, what information will we provide to each other, what issues do we expect to be involved in and informed of?

❑ **What boundaries are there?** In any organization there are limits to an individual's ability to take decisions – the organization's strategy, resources, governance, and so on. An open discussion of these boundaries will help people to understand the limitations without giving up their ability and responsibility to make choices within those boundaries.

❑ **Where can you relax your operating mechanisms?** Regular meetings, approvals, reporting, and escalation are the "carriers of control." Discuss what the right balance is for your new level of capability and mutual confidence.

❑ **What aspects of the manager's job could the individual now take over?** As an individual at this stage you should be asking: "What else can I do to earn the right to be even more empowered?" and "What part of my boss's job would I like to take more responsibility for?" This may lead to development plans in new areas where the leader needs to help the individual develop the capability and confidence to be successful – while making sure they do not interfere in the areas where the individual is already fully capable and confident.

MOVING BEYOND EMPOWERMENT TO FREEDOM

Freedom is actually a bigger game than power. Power is about what you can control. Freedom is about what you can unleash.
Harriet Rubin, publisher and author, USA

So far you have been practicing conditional freedom. You have been checking that people have the capability and that you have mutual confidence before you allow higher levels of autonomy. This is an appropriate style to use with new people who are still learning about the job or the organization.

However, conditional freedom carries within it the assumption that managers hold power by right and that they should make the choices about what should be delegated and empowered. It is the manager's choice to give away that power and that task and therefore they remain the primary person accountable for it.

A more radical next step is to flip the assumption. Let's assume that the individual has freedom by right, that the norm is that we trust people to perform.

Your ability to implement this thinking will be shaped by your own confidence and by the corporate culture in which you are operating. You may be uncomfortable in going so far, but the further you can push in this direction, the higher the levels of autonomy, engagement, and accountability you will release in your people.

In this phase you are looking for the individual to take ownership of their own role. True accountability starts with goal and role setting. Freely chosen commitments are much more likely to lead to high levels of engagement, accountability, and achievement.

Individuals at this stage should be proposing their own goals and starting to shape those roles in accordance with their understanding of the needs of the job and their personal aspirations. We should encourage people to choose broader accountabilities than the span of resources they control, so that their roles become wider and they need to explore new opportunities and engage with colleagues.

Leaders then become a resource to a fully capable and confident individual. Leaders help create the context or environment for success and are available for support, when asked.

We had a choice: we could either trust no one until they proved they were trustworthy and capable (guilty until proven innocent) or we could start by trusting everybody until something happens that shows we were wrong (innocent until proven guilty). In a very small number of cases the latter approach goes wrong, but in the vast majority of cases our trust is reconfirmed. The alternative would be to treat the 95 percent of trustworthy people in an untrustworthy way. That didn't seem to make sense.

R&D manager, healthcare, USA

It takes discipline for a leader only to get involved when asked. It can be difficult to implement this in an environment in which senior leaders expect managers to know everything that's going on in their area of responsibility. You will need to set up an information system to ensure that you have the level of communication and involvement you need to be successful in your corporate culture.

After I used the coaching technique to demonstrate to my production managers that they could solve problems for themselves, the number of telephone calls I received at home declined until eventually they didn't call me at all.

A couple of times I was asked questions by senior managers that I could not answer and it was clear that they felt I should know more about what was going on. I was confident in the ability of my production managers to manage, but the expectations of the rest of the business were different.

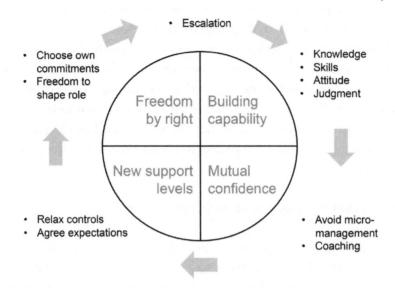

- Escalation

- Choose own
  commitments
- Freedom to
  shape role

Freedom
by right

Building
capability

- Knowledge
- Skills
- Attitude
- Judgment

New support
levels

Mutual
confidence

- Relax controls
- Agree expectations

- Avoid micro-
  management
- Coaching

Figure 14.1   Continuous improvement process for people development

I agreed on two rules with my production managers. If the problem involved an accident, or an incident that might appear in the press the next day, I wanted to be informed straight away. The rest could wait.

The freedom principle turns the issue of delegation and empowerment on its head. Now authority is naturally held at the lowest possible level and delegated upward only at the request of empowered people.

While few organizations really work this way as yet, it does have a strong appeal in principle and does seem to lead to higher levels of engagement and performance. The further we can move toward the principle of empowerment by right, the faster we can react and the less we will need managers to be accessible 24 hours a day.

If people abuse the assumption of autonomy by making poor-quality decisions or judgments, this can be dealt with by exception. We do not need to treat everyone as if they are idiots, just because a small minority may be.

The leader still needs to stay engaged with individuals and look for opportunities to add value when requested, but they should not be taking responsibility or control away from those who are capable and confident enough to do things for themselves.

Leaders will know that an individual has reached the limits of their capability and confidence when they feel the need to escalate again. If a new problem emerges or the environment has changed, the phone will start to ring. This is the leader's signal to begin the process again by making sure that the individual has the capability to solve the problem for themselves next time – and the process continues.

Culture, micromanagement, and empowerment

Both national and corporate cultures have a major impact on the nature of control and empowerment. Cultures that traditionally give higher levels of deference to hierarchy and bureaucracy may consider that these are more effective ways to operate than empowerment.

However, in a complex, particularly global, matrix, the hierarchical and bureaucratic model can be much less effective. Senior individuals may not be the experts in local cultures and conditions and may be unable to make the best or the fastest decisions. Escalation always introduces additional cost and delay.

If you operate within a national or organizational culture that emphasizes control and hierarchy, it can take much more management courage and discipline to manage the transition to the way of working that I am recommending. It will require top-down change and modeling of these behaviors from your most senior leaders.

In cultures that value bureaucracy or are highly regulated, managers will have to distinguish clearly between areas where bureaucratic controls are necessary or even mandatory and those where higher levels of empowerment can lead to increased speed and effectiveness.

I believe that a more decentralized and empowered form of operation is most effective in creating engagement and performance in a matrix, but I do recognize that the journey there may differ depending on your corporate or national culture and your operating mechanisms.

Use the information in this chapter to create a closed-loop continuous improvement process for your people. It is simple, but if you do it systematically you will be continuously developing and empowering people and pushing autonomy down to the lowest possible levels in the organization.

By doing this, you activate some powerful drivers of engagement: work becomes more meaningful, you build higher levels of confidence and trust, people learn and develop continuously, and they feel recognized by achieving higher levels of autonomy.

Before you leave this chapter

❏ Have your people got the capability to deliver and perform?
❏ Have you identified what issues are escalated to you and put plans in place so that people can solve issues for themselves in the future?
❏ Are you confident in people's ability to fulfill their role?
❏ Do you recognize any of the micromanagement traps in yourself?
- Focusing on problem solving rather than people development.
- Not having confidence in your people to execute effectively.
- Having too a high a need for personal control.
❏ Are your people confident to take on more autonomy?
❏ Do you use nondirective coaching to increase empowerment?
❏ Have you relaxed support levels to reflect the capability and confidence of your people?
❏ Have you challenged your people to take more responsibility in defining their own goals and roles?

15

Building, Maintaining, and Repairing Trust

A precondition for decentralized control

Since I wrote about the importance of trust in complex companies in *Speed Lead* in 2005, there has been an explosion of interest in trust as an academic subject and as a management practice. High levels of trust are one of the primary drivers of employee engagement.

In this chapter I will summarize the current thinking on trust and then concentrate on the particular issues of building trust in complex, matrix organizations. The chapter covers:

❏ What we know about trust
❏ The challenges of building trust in a matrix
❏ The three phases of trust in matrix and virtual teams

WHAT WE KNOW ABOUT TRUST

It is a big thing

The level of trust in a team or organization directly correlates with retention, job performance, innovation, job satisfaction, and commitment to decisions and is particularly important at times of change. Most managers I meet do not need convincing of the value of trust.

In our training programs we ask people to stand up if they have ever worked in an environment where trust was low. Usually about a quarter of the group have had that experience.

When they stand up we ask them to remember how it felt. You can actually see their body language change. Their shoulders slump, their faces take on a pained expression, and you can feel the energy being drained from them just at the memory.

Trust is like the air we breathe. When it is present, nobody really notices. But when it is absent, everybody notices.
Warren Buffett, investor and philanthropist, USA

Trust reduces transaction costs

Teams and organizations with high levels of trust spend less time and money on checking and protecting themselves. People are more willing to share information and to learn. Trust increases willingness and confidence to take risks, to deal with ambiguity, and to be creative.

Trust and control are deeply interrelated

The less we trust people, the more we tend to control them. The higher the level of control, the lower the level of trust that people feel. As a result, trust is essential to true delegation, empowerment, and freedom and enables the decentralized decision making that is essential in a matrix.

Trust is about capability and character

People pay attention to both:

❏ **Capability** is about whether you are reliable. Do you have the skills and do you deliver what you say you will?
❏ **Character** is about whether your behavior is predictable, consistent, open, and fair? Do you have integrity and share the organization's values, and do you care about others' wellbeing?

Trust operates at different levels

Each of us has different levels of trust in ourselves, in others, in groups, in organizations, and even in society as a whole. As an individual, our level of trust will be affected by our character and by our experiences at all of these levels: the part of the world we live in, the kind of organization we work in, our colleagues, and our personal propensities and experiences.

In this chapter I will focus on creating trust with individuals in groups and teams. Most trust issues that managers can influence directly are caused by problems between individuals.

Give trust first

If we assume distrust to begin with, we will often start a negative spiral and create what we initially feared. It is good practice to extend trust first. By doing this, we are most likely to initiate a positive, trusting relationship. Occasionally we will be disappointed, so trust does imply a certain amount of risk taking.

Trust assumes vulnerability

If I ask people whether they trust their colleagues, they often ask "to do what?" The trust required to work effectively in a virtual team is clearly different than that required to let someone look after your children. Trust is both more important and more difficult to give when you feel vulnerable or at risk. "Thin trust" – the general assumption that people will cooperate – can be built much more quickly than "thick trust" – the knowledge that I can rely on you when things are really difficult. In many business situations, thin trust is enough.

THE CHALLENGES OF BUILDING TRUST IN A MATRIX

In a matrix we have additional challenges because we need to build trust across five key barriers: distance, cultures, time zones, technology, and organizational complexity.

Distance

Distance means that we have limited face-to-face time. In single-site operations, trust tends to be a free by-product of proximity. People get to know each other and form personal relationships over coffee and lunch. They meet each other's families and build common interests. The traditional mechanisms of trust building require face-to-face time together. We know from working in virtual teams that even emails improve after a face-to-face meeting.

Because we have a limited chance to evaluate character and personality, when we evaluate trustworthiness in remote colleagues we focus more on capability and the willingness to respond. I may not know you as a person, but I can quickly see how you respond to my email.

Since the opportunities to evaluate trustworthiness face to face are fewer, and usually shorter, we need to pay great attention to them. When we meet, we must make sure that we give people the chance to build trust and get to know one another, not simply listen to PowerPoint presentations.

Cultures

Cultural differences can have a major impact on trust. People tend to form relationships fastest with people who are similar to them. They also attribute more trustworthy behaviors in the early stages of trust formation to people from their own "in group."

Different cultures have different expectations about what it takes to develop and maintain a relationship. People can be disappointed when unspoken assumptions are not met.

Our US colleagues are surprisingly open and friendly. They use first names quickly and talk about things that we might not openly discuss except with close friends. They behave as if they want to be our friends, but then if there is a problem or something that is not strictly in their job description, they tend not to reply to requests and may even break the relationship. In Asia, we tend to stick with our friends, particularly when things are tough.

Localization manager, software, Japan

Language and cultural differences can cause misunderstandings that create delay or undermine trust. Is that very direct email from your German colleague rude, or is it merely an example of the direct professional communication that is normal in Germany? Is that very indirect email from your English colleague polite or deliberately evasive?

A shared language and context help trust grow more quickly within an in-group that shares the same context – they watch the same television shows and laugh at the same jokes. Unfortunately, this can further exclude people from outside the cultural group.

Time zones

Time zones lead to delays and limit communication opportunities. When you have an urgent problem and your colleague does not reply, is that because they are not cooperating, or because they are asleep? Even in the best situations, time zones mean that we have to wait for a response, which can often mean waiting until the next working day.

Conference calls that are routinely held at inconvenient times and late-night or early-morning calls at home can all cause trust issues in global teams.

Technology

Communicating through technology can lead to misunderstandings when we don't grasp the content or tone of messages.

However, there is some evidence that communicating by text can mitigate some of the effects of cultural misunderstandings and in-group problems in the early stage of trust formation, by breaking down language barriers and leveling the playing field in communication and forming relationships.

Organizational complexity

As I have stressed throughout this book, organizations today are much more dynamic and flexible. We work with colleagues across functional barriers, with multiple reporting lines, in virtual teams, joint ventures, alliances, and complex relationships that cannot be precisely regulated through contracts and rules. The more we experience dynamism, change, and uncertainty, the more we need trust.

But as we have seen, competing goals, unclear roles, lack of alignment, and complex forms of cooperation and control can all create ambiguity and potentially undermine trust.

The greater the pace of change and environmental uncertainty, the more we need trust, but the harder it will be to build, maintain, and repair. In order to trust people we need them to be consistent and predictable in their responses; trust requires stability. However, at the same time the less stability there is in the environment, the more we need trust.

For these reasons, building trust is a particular challenge in complex teams and matrix organizations and we need to put it much higher on our management agenda. Trust is no longer a free by-product of proximity.

THE THREE PHASES OF TRUST IN MATRIX AND VIRTUAL TEAMS

There are three key phases in building trust in matrix and virtual teams:

1. Building trust.
2. Maintaining trust as teams mature.
3. Recovering from a breach of trust.

In this section I will look at the practical steps that team members and leaders can take to accelerate the development of trust in each phase.

Phase 1: Building trust

The trust-formation phase is critical, because the behavioral patterns that a team or organization develops are set early in the process.

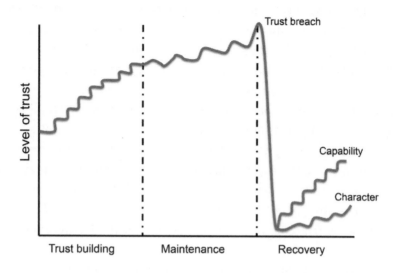

Figure 15.1   The three phases of trust building

After SC Currall & MJ Epstein (2003) The fragility of organizational trust, *Organizational Dynamics*, 32: 193–206.

The perceptions that form at this early stage become a filter through which subsequent interactions are evaluated. If there is initial distrust, future actions will be seen through that lens and perceptions are hard to change.

Virtual teams are not good at reestablishing relationship norms once they are set, so we need to get this right at the beginning.

When we ask individuals on our workshops to estimate how many of the people they typically meet they would consider to be trustworthy, we get answers ranging from 25 percent to 80 percent or more. These are people who work in the same organization, but their propensity to trust is wildly different. This difference is shaped by an individual's personality and life experiences.

In most cases, people believe that those inside their own company are more trustworthy than the general population. Where they do not, this indicates a serious problem within the organization.

When bringing a new member into a team or organization, the manager has a critical role in establishing the initial level of trust. By ascribing trust to the individual, even before they arrive, this can help set the pattern for the future.

In virtual teams this can take the form of an introductory email and photograph from the manager, telling people about the new person's history and achievements. It will certainly involve managing the introductions and getting a new person face to face with team members as quickly as possible.

In my global team we meet face to face twice per year. When a new individual joins we try and get them to start as close as possible to a team meeting, so that one of the very early interactions with new colleagues is face to face. We also try and do some kind of community-building event, so that very quickly they are doing something memorable such as white-water rafting with their new teammates.

CEO, global consulting, UK

We have access to an internal Facebook system, so if a new person joins us from elsewhere in the organization, we can quickly connect to their profile pages and get a lot of information about their work background, but also their hobbies and families. It enables you to identify common interests and people you both know. You feel as though you are getting to know them even before you meet face to face.

Director, internal communications, telecoms, Singapore

As part of induction to a matrix or virtual team, we need to make sure that wherever possible people have the opportunity to spend time with colleagues to get to know them. Relationships and networks are critical to success, so their establishment should be both explicit in an individual's goals and supported by their manager or mentor, who can help them develop the networks necessary to be successful in their new roles.

When putting together a virtual team, trust does not start at zero. Most people come into a work team with a medium to high amount of trust (depending on your organizational culture). If trust does start at zero and has to be built from the ground up each time, then you have a problem.

We call the first phase the "staircase of trust." In this phase we start to work together and look at how others respond. People pay attention to both capability and character – whether you are reliable and deliver and how you behave.

In working with this model around the world, our participants think that there are differences in the balance of how much we pay attention to each of these factors:

❑ In Asia, capability is important but people probably pay closer attention to character in the early stages. The initial level of trust of strangers may be lower, but personal interactions can make it grow fast.

❑ In the USA, people pay closer attention to capability and assume a higher level of initial trust.

❑ Europe is somewhere in the middle, with a moderate assumption of initial trust and a balance between capability and character.

Of course these are very broad generalizations, but most of our participants seem to feel that this matches their experience of working with colleagues from other regions.

Because this phase is characterized by a number of steps, we need to organize the work so that the steps can occur quickly. The most powerful thing we can do to build trust initially is to create quick wins. If the goals of the team are structured so that we do not see whether we have succeeded for six months, then it is a long time before we can tell whether our colleagues really delivered and be ready to take the next trust step.

For this reason, it is important to create collaborative goals where individuals and small subteams, as well as the whole team, can be successful together. This also creates opportunities for celebration and recognition, which are useful tools for creating high levels of trust.

When bringing in new team members, remember to create opportunities for them to demonstrate their capability and character at an early stage.

When I am adding a new member to my virtual team, I always look for some element of value that they bring to the team: some skill, capability, or perspective that the existing team lacks. I get them to train other individuals in the team or join an activity where they can quickly demonstrate their added value.

Successful virtual teams focus on getting on with the work and discussing what needs to be done and how. They have little experience of working with each other, but are normally willing to give people the benefit of the doubt.

If trust is an issue at the first meeting then that is a concern, probably caused by past breaches of trust. Too much focus on trust issues at too early a stage may get in the way by suggesting a problem that you do not really have. Concentrate on succeeding together and you will probably never have a trust problem.

Bringing in a new manager

When a new manager joins a team there are additional challenges. Team members will want to get one-on-one time with the manager as quickly as possible. The manager will also inherit a set of expectations and ways of working from their predecessor and will need to become aware of these quickly.

If the manager is an existing employee of the company, then the team may have preconceptions about them before they even begin. It is good practice to discuss these and to build an open and honest dialogue right from the start. GE has a specific, facilitated process for doing this.

> *Without the manager present, a facilitator meets with the team to come up with questions: What do we already know about the new manager or would like to know? Nothing is off-limits but questions are captured anonymously.*
>
> *The facilitator then meets with the manager to review the issues and the manager responds in front of the team. The meeting goes on to discuss any questions or issues raised and propose any actions necessary.*
>
> GE new manager assimilation process

The pressure on a new manager to make fast changes is usually counterproductive. It is also irritating for both sides to hear either "this is how we did it at my previous company" (from the manager) or "it is just the way we do things around here" (from the team members). Take some time to see how the team operates. Ask open questions about ways of working and understand the culture before you jump in with changes.

Phase 2: Maintaining trust as teams mature

In this phase, initial assumptions and goodwill are replaced by personal experience and a history of interactions. It is the quality of these ongoing interactions that is critical to maintaining long-term trust.

In order to build trust, we need to create more points of social connection as well as business relationships. In most cultures encouraging self-disclosure is helpful to get people to learn more about each other.

Since we have been using an internal Facebook group for project managers, an interesting side-effect has been that we tend to share more about our hobbies, things we are involved in outside the team and even outside work.

These give us a reason to have a conversation which isn't purely about task and this really helps build relationships.

Project manager, insurance, UK

Several of us have been working together for over 10 years and, although we know each other well, it is easy to fall out of the habit of asking people about the rest of their lives. At our face-to-face meetings we use a technique called "good news posters." We each have a flipchart. In the top half we share images and words on the subject "good news at work," on the bottom half we share "good news at home." It is a good way to connect back in on how things are going with their families, hobbies, etc. and we always learn something new.

VP, consulting, USA

An easy trap to fall into in virtual teams is only to call when we have a problem or we need something, and that is not the best way to manage goodwill and trust in a relationship.

Technology can help to keep the heartbeat of communication going. Successful distributed teams establish a rhythm of regular communication events that give structure to the interactions of the team and hold it together. This should include opportunities for those virtual "water-cooler moments" that cement trust through regular small-scale communication.

> *First thing in the morning I can see on Instant Messenger which of my colleagues in Asia are online. I will drop them a quick "how was your day?" message. Most of the time the response is a quick "good thanks, how is yours going?" but sometimes they will message back "are you free for a call?" It keeps the communication flowing. To me it is a bit like meeting someone in the corridor and saying "how are you?"*
>
> Operations manager, IT, business services, Germany

Critically, communication needs to be two way; lots of push-style communication in the form of newsletters, business updates, and emails is not enough. One of the key drivers of engagement is the existence of real two-way conversations, not just one-way broadcasts.

At this maintenance stage, it is important to establish an equitable share of communication. Teams that have trust problems tend to be characterized by only one or two people dominating the communication. Individuals with trust issues will often disengage from communication.

We should also recognize that there can be negative consequences of too much trust. We get significant benefits when trust increases – up to a point. Blind trust, complacency, and personal obligations that stop necessary change happening can all get in the way if there is too much trust.

Probably the most important technique to keep trust developing during this mature stage is to look for opportunities to give away more control. As we saw in Chapter 14, if we keep developing more

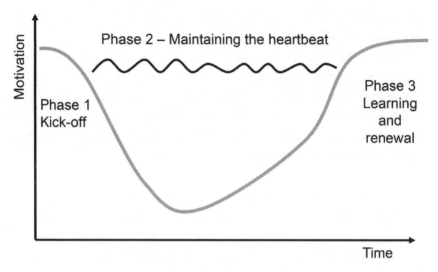

Figure 15.2 The community decay curve

capable and confident individuals and teams but we do not give them more autonomy, then we will create frustration.

It is normal for virtual teams to experience what I called in *Speed Lead* the "community decay curve." Motivation and trust levels start high at the kickoff, when people are enthusiastic and keen to contribute. Trust can wane in the middle of the process, when people are involved in doing the work and are often working individually and remotely. Finally, at the end of the process, when we come together to celebrate success and to recognize contribution, trust and motivation are usually on a high again.

Even the highest-performing teams will have ups and downs in trust. We can use the kickoff process at the beginning and the focus on celebration and recognition at the end to create high points and to reenergize our teams. In many global teams we may only meet face to face once a year and a good practice then is to celebrate the previous year before moving on to kick off the next year's activities.

More regular milestones can give an opportunity for a number of mini-kickoffs and mini-celebrations during the year. Use these tactically to maintain trust levels in the team.

As a manager, it is also important for you to be alert to the small signals of distrust. If you can pick up little issues early and make sure that they are resolved, then they never develop into major issues. These signals can be hard to read remotely and it is useful to develop an environment in your team where individuals can let you know if they become aware of issues that you may not necessarily see from your position.

Phase 3: Recovering from a breach of trust

Trust is easier to destroy than to build. Just one incident of untrustworthy behavior can do it. Trust levels can fall far lower than the position from which the team started. You then have to put a huge amount of effort into just getting back to where you started, and sometimes that may not even be possible.

Most breaches of trust are minor, but if they are not dealt with the perception can become bigger than the reality. After a breach of trust people are hypersensitive to future actions, and they become even more critical of potential trust problems.

Be careful at this stage that people have realistic expectations about certainty. In fast-changing environments, things change and events that can undermine trust may be unavoidable. If individuals are intolerant of realistic levels of uncertainty, they may not be capable of succeeding in a complex working environment.

So what do you do if a breach of trust happens?

❏ **Acknowledge the problem and the feelings around it.** To solve a problem you have to acknowledge that it exists, and many teams dance around trust issues between individuals. Everyone knows they exist, but they are hard to confront. Being clear about it and exploring the parties' facts and feelings around the situation is an essential first step. Ideally, this should be done between the two individuals who have the problem. If they cannot fix it, then the manager or a mediator needs to be involved.

❏ **Involve a trusted adviser to gain some perspective.** People tend to recall clearly the many little things they personally have done to build trust, but they only really notice the big things that others have done to undermine it. There tends to be an emotional reaction based on the feeling that individuals have put a huge amount of effort into building trust and then been let down. This needs to be understood from the perspective of the injured party. A third party can help build perspective for both individuals if the manager is not able to do so.

❏ **Acknowledge your role.** The person who is at fault should accept responsibility explicitly and either offer to make amends or show a desire to reach a reconciliation.

❏ **Let it go and move on.** Trust is never completely destroyed if both parties want to continue the relationship.

I strongly recommended that efforts to rebuild trust are initiated face to face or at least using a technology with a visual element, such as video conferencing. It is hard to do these things through email.

For more serious conflicts, you may want to use the conflict-management sequence in Chapter 8.

Again, the difference between character and capability matters here. If an individual works hard and tries their best but fails because they didn't have the skills or capability, then we will tend to forgive them. We want to make sure that they receive training or other capability building first, but then we can resume building the staircase of trust.

However, if an individual shows a failure of character or integrity, this is much harder to recover from. Even if the individual now acts with integrity for an extended period, at the back of our minds we still know that they are capable of acting without integrity.

In virtual teams, it is much harder to recover from a character problem than a capability problem. We have many opportunities to demonstrate capability and reliability, but few opportunities to demonstrate convincingly that we have changed our character.

In cross-cultural teams we need to be careful about attributing meaning to the behaviors we observe. Check that what you are interpreting as a character problem is not simply a cultural difference by getting some local cultural advice.

In virtual teams, where you may have little management control over individuals and perhaps only have them working on your teams for a small part of their time, I am pessimistic about the ability to change fundamental character issues.

In my corporate career, particularly my time in industrial relations and HR, I was involved in a large number of recruitment interviews, performance management reviews, and disciplinary issues. In all that time I can only think of one example when an individual significantly changed their character at work. It may be more practical to get the individual off the team than to try to change them.

The challenge, of course, is to be sure that you are talking about a character issue; it may be a matter of behavior, which can change. If it is really a matter of a mismatch in deeply held values, then you probably need to find a way to get the individual out of the team.

A final point on rebuilding trust. If a trust problem is between individuals, treat it as an individual problem and do not try to use a team workshop to solve it. It is very frustrating for team members who do not have any difficulties to be held accountable for solving an issue between two individuals. It is the manager's job to make sure that this is sorted out, ideally by the people involved themselves.

Trust from a management perspective

Managers have a special place in building trust.

Managers have the responsibility for taking the first step by giving and demonstrating trust, particularly as they have a position of power in the relationship.

When managers evaluate the trustworthiness of their people, they tend to focus on the competence and reliability of their subordinates and the willingness or effort that they put into complying with requests.

Individuals tend to pay more attention to character issues when evaluating their managers. They have some level of dependence on their manager, and so they spend much more time studying and analyzing the manager's behaviors and motivations.

As managers we need to make sure that we are:

❏ Continually developing the capability and confidence in the team and looking for opportunities to give away control and build increased engagement, accountability, and autonomy.

❏ Explicit about norms, ensuring that there are regular discussions and negotiations to develop clear mutual expectations (trust can be undermined if unspoken assumptions are not met).

❏ Accessible – in global teams it is important to discuss what is reasonable in terms of accessibility. People do not need you to be around the whole time; in fact, they appreciate the freedom of not having the boss looking over their shoulder. But they do want you to be accessible when they need you. You should discuss with your team what accessibility means: is it OK to call you at home, and at what hours?

Managers face dilemmas around trust: there are certain things that are part of the management role but that may undermine trust. To an extent, having a manager at all is already an admission that people need to be "managed" rather than trusted to do the right things.

Sometimes managers are put into positions where their obligations to the organization conflict with their obligations to their people, particularly when they are required to cut costs or manage downsizing. Generally speaking, followers understand that managers have relatively little discretion in these areas, and where managers have to take this kind of action it does not reflect badly on their trustworthiness, provided that they do it with integrity.

A good mantra for all of us is: "Say what you will do, do what you say, explain if it changes."

Trust is one of the most important drivers of employee engagement and as we have seen in this chapter, the matrix brings some additional challenges in this area. We need to organize for trust if it is to happen systematically.

Use the information in this chapter to bring trust onto your management agenda. Evaluate the trust levels in your team and put in place specific actions to build, maintain, or repair trust as necessary.

Before you leave this chapter

❏ Is the trust strong enough in your team or organization?
❏ What are the factors that can undermine trust in your team?
❏ Where is your matrix team in the process of trust building:
  • Formation?
  • Maintenance?
  • Recovery?
❏ What can you do to build trust at this phase of your team's development?

Part IV
The Matrix
Mindset and Skillset

In Part IV I will return to the key theme of this book: the importance of building the matrix mindset, the attitudes and approach that bring success in this more complex environment.

In order to adopt and practice this mindset, people need the right supporting skills. Without a new skillset, they will naturally fall back on traditional management techniques, which may be counterproductive in the matrix.

I will also identify the skills required for leaders, for collaboration, and for personal effectiveness in the matrix.

In Part IV:

Chapter 16   The matrix mindset and skillset – be a matrix manager, not a matrix victim

The Matrix
Mindset and Skillset

Be a matrix manager,
not a matrix victim

The key challenge in matrix success is creating a mindset and a skillset in our people that allow them to cope with the new level of complexity.

This mindset and skillset are very different from those established in stable and relatively simple environments, where managers had all the answers and cause and effect were relatively clear.

Throughout the book I have given examples of two types of attitude: the matrix victim and the matrix manager. The matrix manager does not have to be managing other people; they may merely be managing themselves.

The matrix victim harks back to a simpler (and perhaps illusory) past, where managers thought they had all the answers and cascaded clarity, authority, and responsibility down from on high.

If I ask participants in our training programs to define what they expect from a leader, they come up with a list of criteria that could only be fulfilled by a visionary CEO who is also head of a major world religion! I always ask them: "If your leader does all these things, what is left for you to do?"

All the research I have seen says that people want more autonomy, more freedom and responsibility at work. At the same time, we have the unrealistic expectation that our leaders have all the answers.

In a matrix, where we have multiple bosses, you may be the only individual who has a full view of your own goals, role, and priorities. At best, one of your managers will have half of the picture.

If you are the only person with this full picture and you have the greatest motivation to change, then you need to be active and assertive in fulfilling your communication needs and in owning your goals, role, and skills. This is the matrix mindset.

The matrix victim waits for someone else to bring clarity; the matrix manager relishes the flexibility, autonomy, and breadth that the matrix gives them.

Matrix victim	Matrix manager
My goals are not clear	Here are the commitments I have chosen
I do not have a job description and am not clear what I should be doing	This is what needs doing
I do not have the authority to get things done	Who do I need to influence to get this done?
I cannot be accountable for things I do not control	Where can I get the resources to meet my commitments?
My manager doesn't empower me	What have I done to earn the right to take on more responsibility?

The key elements of the matrix mindset include:

❑ **Self-leadership** – taking control and ownership for your goals, role, and skills. People with the matrix mindset seek out and engage those they need to be successful and push back against unnecessary control from others.
❑ **Breadth** – people who are successful in the matrix think beyond their role and function. They take ownership for the delivery of results that cross organizational boundaries and involve external suppliers or other partners to get things done. They create the networks and relationships necessary to achieve this.
❑ **Being comfortable with ambiguity** – the ability to bring clarity, structure, and control to bear when necessary, coupled with the confidence to move beyond this to work with ambiguity, flexibility, and trust.

❑ **Being adaptive** – flexible and open to learning, new ideas, and new ways of working. People know that today's solution to a dilemma may not be the right solution tomorrow.

❑ **Being influential** – people who do not fall back on traditional power and authority to get things done. They build trust and use a wide range of influence techniques and sources of power. They see recourse to hierarchy as a failure.

This mindset needs to reflect the reality of leading people and working with colleagues across barriers of distance, cultures, time zones, organizational complexity, and communications technology.

For the most senior leaders, those who sit at the top of a matrix, the situation may not have changed so much. They still have high levels of positional power and are probably already used to working in this broad, autonomous, and adaptive way.

If this is you, think about how you developed this mindset and the time you have taken to create your networks, socialize ideas with your peers, and learn to deal with ambiguity. In a matrix we are asking people much further down the organization to exhibit the same skills in leading themselves and others and in managing complex dilemmas and tradeoffs.

Senior leaders have a vital role in creating the climate in which the matrix middle can succeed. If we do not give these individuals the skills, information, and authority to manage in this way, then you can expect to see high levels of escalation.

Senior leaders can also help "demystify the matrix" by communicating clearly the reasons for the structure; by providing resources to build the new communities, networks, teams, and groups we need; by modeling the mindset; and by acting quickly to resolve escalations, bottlenecks, and challenges in the operation of the structure.

The matrix will also challenge some of our traditional skillsets and assumptions about management. We need to make sure that our reward and recognition processes reinforce rather than undermine the matrix mindset and we need to build the new skills necessary for success.

The development of the matrix skillset is a critical underpinning of the building of the matrix mindset. If managers do not have the concepts, tools, and skills necessary to be successful in a matrix, then they will fall back on using the tools and approaches that they applied in the past. We need an alternative set of skills if we want to see a different outcome.

As we have seen, our traditional management preoccupation with teamwork, control, and increased communication can all be counter-productive in getting things done in the matrix.

Matrix success requires new skills at three levels: leadership, collaboration, and personal effectiveness.

Leadership

People who are responsible for leading others in the matrix need to learn how to:

❏ Demystify the matrix for their people.
❏ Build clarity and organizational alignment.
❏ Streamline cooperation.
❏ Create and support accountability without control.
❏ Communicate effectively to diverse groups and through technology.
❏ Exercise power and influence without authority.
❏ Lead others toward empowerment and freedom.
❏ Find the right balance of trust and control.
❏ Build a culture that supports matrix working.

Collaboration

People responsible for establishing and running teams, groups, communities, and networks need to understand what is different in:

❏ Building and aligning team goals.
❏ Managing competing goals and priorities within the team.
❏ Choosing and using spaghetti teams, star groups, cloud communities, and purposeful networks.
❏ Building matrix teams – creating, improving, and running teams across barriers of distance, cultures, time zones, technology, and organizational complexity.

❏ Supporting cooperation through technology – creating relevance in communication and building participation and engagement online.
❏ Building, maintaining, and repairing trust in the matrix environment.
❏ Managing team celebration and learning remotely.

Personal effectiveness

Individuals within a matrix need to build the skills to:

❏ Define and clarify their own goals.
❏ Manage alignment with others.
❏ Deal with competing goals and higher levels of ambiguity.
❏ Own and shape their own role.
❏ Manage multiple bosses and divided loyalties.
❏ Build and engage a matrix network to get things done.
❏ Manage tradeoffs, choices, and dilemmas.
❏ Influence without authority.
❏ Build trust with colleagues across distance and cultures.
❏ Escalate positively.
❏ Manage conflict.
❏ Communicate through technology.
❏ Work in matrix, virtual, and global teams.
❏ Work across time zones.
❏ Stay visible when working remotely.

If you are in HR, learning and development, or organizational development, you can support your matrix by making sure that your selection, training provision, goal setting, and reward strategies reflect the matrix mindset and skillset.

If we do not build this new skillset and mindset, individuals will be applying behaviors and skills that are not adapted to the level of complexity of the matrix and that may well be counterproductive.

If we get this right, however, the matrix mindset enables us to create some powerful new opportunities for increasing employee engagement. Yes, the matrix is more complex and can be confusing;

but it also brings opportunities for much broader and more meaningful work, higher levels of role ownership and autonomy, and a much richer environment for learning.

The matrix may not be for everyone, but for those who can develop the matrix mindset and the supporting skillset there are real opportunities for more fulfilling and engaging work.

In the words of a senior manager on one of our matrix training programs: "A matrix can be a web you get caught in or a network you use to get things done." Which of these it is for you will depend not on your structure, but on whether you develop your own mindset and skillset for matrix success. Good luck!

You can see more videos, podcasts, and articles about our matrix leadership, matrix teams, and matrix working training, or contact us to discuss your specific challenges at www.global-integration.com. You can also join our LinkedIn "Matrix Management" group or follow @GlobalInteg on Twitter to raise questions, share your experiences about using the tools in the book, stay up to date with new developments, or join the conversation.

Before you leave this chapter

❏ When you recruit people for matrix roles, do you look for the matrix mindset?

❏ What evidence can you collect during recruitment about people's past experience of operating this way?

❏ Are you rewarding successful matrix behaviors through your recognition and career-development systems?

❏ Do individuals in your organization have the skills necessary to be successful in the matrix?

❏ Do your training and development support people in building the matrix skillset?

Acknowledgments

To my colleagues at Global Integration – Tony Poots, Phil Stockbridge, John Bland, Rod Farnan, Janet Davis, Tim Mitchell, T.H. Ong, Robyn Green, Caroline Blair, Claire Thompson, and Laura Hall. Thanks for your ideas, input, and challenges and for heading off some of my wilder ideas.

To our hundreds of clients and tens of thousands of participants around the world – thank you for sharing your problems, ideas, and stories and for constantly challenging us to make our tools practical and actionable.

Thanks also to Nick Brealey and his team at Nicholas Brealey Publishing for all your help in bringing this book to life; it seemed a bit less painful this time.

Index

ABOUT GLOBAL INTEGRATION

Global Integration is a global ideas, training, and consulting group specializing in matrix management, virtual teams, and global working. We have worked with over 300 of the world's leading organizations since 1994 and have delivered over 100,000 participant days of training in these topics in more than 40 countries.

Our clients come to us for five key reasons:

❑ **We are specialists** – we focus on matrix management, virtual teams, and global working exclusively and are thought leaders in these fields. You can see more about our ideas on our website.

❑ **We provide real business benefits** – teams and organizations who use our services deliver faster, at lower cost, and with higher levels of employee confidence and satisfaction.

❑ **We are credible** – our people are all experienced facilitators and have all been line managers in major multinationals. We work with the world's leading companies and our tools and techniques have been validated around the world.

❑ **We can deliver globally** – we operate from hubs in Europe, North America, and Asia and regularly run training events around the world.

❑ **We are easy to work with** – we are passionate about cutting through complexity and creating mutual relationships with our customers.

If you recognize some of the challenges in this book, why not contact us to find out more about the solutions to your specific issues? We can provide training and other services, face to face or through technology, around the world in a range of languages.

Find out more or contact us through www.global-integration.com, join our LinkedIn "Matrix Management" group, or follow @GlobalInteg on Twitter to keep in touch with developments and join the conversation.

Also by Kevan Hall
from Nicholas Brealey Publishing

SPEED LEAD
Faster, Simpler Ways to Manage People, Projects and Teams in Complex Companies

The antidote to corporate complexity, *Speed Lead* describes tried-and-tested techniques for making companies faster, easier to run and more satisfying for everyone involved.

In his work with hundreds of the world's leading companies, including Microsoft, Vodafone and Nokia, Kevan Hall has discovered that up to 50% of time is wasted in most offices, and that talented people spend more than 80% of their time on cooperation, communication and control in the workplace.

Speed Lead incorporates this knowledge and Hall's experience of consulting and training more than 35,000 people in over 200 of the world's leading companies in order to combat these issues. His challenging but ultimately practical ideas have enabled organizations to significantly reduce international activity and project cycle times, build close international business relationships and curb the costs of unnecessary travel and expensive communication.

Unravel the complexity of your corporation and utilize some of Hall's key principles, such as abolishing "bored" meetings and allowing your employees to make "good enough" decisions on their own. *Speed Lead* will have you on the fast track to streamlined business practices in no time!

Hardcover
ISBN 978-1-857883-74-9, eISBN 978-1-85788-499-9
£20.00
www.nicholasbrealey.com